Home
Wine &
Beer
Making

Home Wine & Beer Making

Gladys Mann

Octopus Books

First published 1974 by
Octopus Books Limited
59 Grosvenor Street,
London W1

ISBN 0 7064 0361 4

© 1974 Octopus Books Limited

Produced by
Mandarin Publishers Limited
14 Westlands Road,
Quarry Bay, Hong Kong
Printed in Hong Kong

Contents

Preface

Wine drinking has increased enormously over the past ten years, partly because wine has become more easily available; partly because of increased travel to the traditional wine producing countries bordering the Mediterranean; and partly because of the growing availability of home wine makers' equipment.

Home wine making is so easy today that a great number of families have taken up the art in order to enjoy their own wines with their meals, their own aperitifs and their own liqueurs. The use of wine in cooking has also spread —and, for the home wine maker, all this is available at a fraction of the cost of the highly desirable, but increasingly expensive, wares of the wine merchant.

Wine making by the amateur can no longer be con-

6

sidered as a remote country craft, but for the person who so wishes, and is able, to gather flowers, fruits and vegetables in their season, the opportunity exists for experimenting with a huge variety of new and interesting wines.

The creative spirit of the wine maker can be fully indulged in his hobby and, if he or she joins a local wine makers' club or guild, there will be plenty of opportunity to discuss mutual interests, share difficulties and enjoy social occasions enlightened by a few glasses of wine.

Remember that in most countries the distillation of spirits from wine is illegal; not only does it rob the government of revenue, but certain distillate fractions are poisonous. Neither can home-made wine be sold,

although of course you can give away as much as you like: and what better present?

Making beer—or home brewing as it is often called—is a fast-growing leisure activity, as a quick glance around any health shop or large store will prove, with shelf upon shelf of brewing materials and equipment.

Some people complain that present day commercial beers are being sold on eye-appeal rather than taste, and bemoan the loss of full-flavoured beers. For this reason many people are turning to home brewing as an alternative to mass-produced beers, with the additional incentive that the home produced product is much cheaper.

A selection of home-made wines

Making Wine

Introduction

History

The origins of wine making are lost in the past, although we know that grape vines, and wine making were introduced to the Mediterranean areas by at least 3000 B.C. The craft has flourished there ever since and has extended to most parts of the world wherever the climate is suitable for viniculture.

There has recently been a tremendous revival of wine making. This is largely accounted for by the arrival of canned, concentrated grape and other fruit juices and pulps, so that today's wine maker need travel only to his nearest specialist shop to obtain the simple ingredients that enable excellent wine to be prepared in the most limited surroundings.

Summarized Theory

Wine is a mixture of water and alcohol flavoured by fruit or vegetable juice and other ingredients. In some fruits, notably the grape, the 'other ingredients' occur naturally to a greater or lesser extent; any lack of them will have to be made up artificially.

To make wine, yeast is added to the fruit or vegetable juice; the yeast converts the sugar in the juice into alcohol, and carbon dioxide is given off. When the solution contains about 17% of alcohol, the action of the yeast is inhibited, and if any sugar remains, the wine is sweet. If all the sugar has been converted before this point is reached, the wine is dry. Few natural juices will contain enough sugar to make sweet wine on their own, and in general, sugar has to be added to obtain a sufficient proportion of alcohol. It is better to aim at a dry wine, because it can be sweetened after making if this is desired.

Wine is most easily made from grapes for several reasons. The juice contains a large proportion of sugar, and the flavour is often adequate without additives. Generally, too, grape juice will ferment naturally because 'wild' yeasts are present in the skins or other parts of the vine, and it was doubtless in this way that wine was first made.

Although concentrated grape juices are freely available today, many amateurs wish to try their hand at other types of wine. This book describes how to make wine from virtually any fruit or vegetable that is available.

Wine Classification

Some wines may be broadly described as 'general purpose': a glass in the middle of the morning can be a pick-me-up; the wine may be suitable for cooking; or it may be drunk with lunch or dinner, or used as a basis for 'party wines', usually punches. Tastes differ enormously in wines. Exact classification is therefore to be undertaken with some diffidence, but the broad divisions are generally recognized as follows.

Dream of the pharoah's cup-bearer (left)
An old wine press in Crete (right)

Aperitifs or appetizers, wine based and quite sharp to the taste; in fact, just the thing to get the gastric juices stirring. Sherries are in another category, but are usually drunk as an aperitif.

Table wines cover a wide range and can be of the red or white variety, or any colour in-between. It is found that the lighter, dryer white wines are excellent accompaniments to fish, veal or chicken, while the heavier, fuller-bodied red wines are more suited to dark meats. Do not let tradition or custom put you off, however—there are no rules—drink whatever you most enjoy.

Dessert wines include the ports, muscatels and sweet wines and, at the end of a meal, what is more pleasant than a sweet liqueur with the coffee?

Mead, a traditional old English beverage made from fermented honey, is not in great favour these days, although many wine makers try a brew every now and again. Mead and Cider can be considered as general-purpose drinks for consumption before, during or after a meal, as fancy dictates.

Ancient Egyptians blending wines with syphons (above)

Alcohol Content

The alcohol in wines is measured in % alcohol. Below about 10% alcohol the wine would probably not keep for more than 3 or 4 months, although a low alcohol white wine can make a very pleasant summer drink. Most table wines average between 10 and 12% alcohol, but stronger wines, up to around 17% alcohol, can be made at home quite easily. For higher strength wines, fortification is necessary: that is, the addition of brandy or a tasteless spirit such as vodka.

A variety of glasses and bottles for different types of wine (right)

12

Ingredients and Equipment

Basics

Almost any vegetable matter will ferment and therefore almost any fruit or vegetable, either fresh, dried or as juicy extract, can be used to make wine. There are exceptions, however, which are either downright poisonous or else unpleasant, and these should be avoided. It is always advisable, therefore, to follow the well-known and tried ingredients mentioned in the very many published or personally recommended recipes that one encounters; there is enough variety for everyone's tastes. If you have access to the countryside or possess a garden you may be able to pick many of the items fresh.

These are some of the common home wine makers' ingredients:

Fresh Vegetables—Beetroot, broadbeans, carrots, celery, parsnips, pea pods, parsley.
Flowers—picked fresh—Cowslips, dandelions, elderflowers, hawthorn blossom, marigolds, rose hips, rose petals, primroses.
Grains—Wheat, barley, rice.
Dried Fruits—Apricots, bananas, bilberries, elderberries, dates, grains, elderflowers, figs, nuts, peaches, raisins, rose hips, sloes, sultanas.
Fruit, canned Fruit Juices or Pulps—Apples, apricots, bilberries, cherries, grapefruit, peaches, pineapples, prunes, rhubarb.
Canned Grape Juice—plain red or white, or in many varieties, labelled (hopefully) with the flavours of Burgundy, Bordeaux, Chablis, Sauternes, Vermouth, port, sherry, etc.

Additives

The only other essentials required for most wines are yeast, sugar and water, but for keeping properties and for sterilization of equipment, Campden tablets must be included. Some wines, such as the flower wines, do need a stronger flavour to give them a 'bite'; some yeasts need a yeast nutrient when used with certain juices. Flavouring additives include citric acid, grape tannin, ginger, tartaric acid, and malic acid. Glycerine, a natural constituent of wine, improves the smoothness of some red wines. A pectin-destroying enzyme, such as Pectolase or Pectozyme, inhibits pectin haze, a frequent cause of cloudiness, especially in stone fruit wines.

Yeasts are available in great variety—the granular baker's yeast is very popular since it can be bought in small tins that will serve for many fermentations. Some yeasts of this type are sold in small sachets for 1 to 5 gallons of must, sometimes complete with the yeast nutrient. In addition, there are sachets of special yeasts for special wines and liquid yeasts in variety. They are all worth a try. All of these items are available at the wine maker's shop or chemists, who will always give

Ingredients and equipment for making wine (right)

14

advice on, for example, the many varieties of yeast on the market today.

Ordinary white granulated sugar is the easiest to obtain and use, but invert sugar may assist fermentation in the early stages.

Regarding the water—straight from the cold water tap is adequate in most districts, but some wine makers recommend that where the water is very hard, it should first be boiled and cooled.

Primary Equipment

If you plan to make wine the easy way, with canned juices, all you need to start is a gallon glass or polythene jar, a rubber bung to fit this, a fermentation trap ('bubbler') and a plastic syphon. All of these items are cheap and can be used over and over again. As you expand, you need only buy additional jars, bungs and fermentation traps.

When the time for drinking arrives you will need a few bottles, and corks or plastic stoppers. You will not need very many, because it is easier to store the wine in gallon quantities.

For sterilizing, for preservative qualities and to inhibit further fermentation you will require Campden tablets or sodium metabisulphite (sodium pyrosulphite), a white powder which is the active ingredient of Campden tablets.

The more adventurous, using fresh fruit or vegetables, will need some additional utensils for preparing the juice and will be dealing, usually, in rather larger quantities.

Firstly, a word of warning—avoid containers, spoons or mashers of brass, copper or iron; use only aluminium, unchipped enamel ware or stainless steel in the preparation stages. Do not use lead glazed crocks.

For boiling, a five gallon electric wash boiler is very useful, especially as it does not occupy any of the space on the kitchen stove. Alternatively, use a large saucepan or jam-making can. An electric liquidizer saves a lot of time and trouble, and a large pressure cooker can be useful.

Most ingredients must be 'steeped' and for this purpose the large glazed bread or egg preserving crock is suitable, but rather easier to obtain today is a plastic dustbin.

The fermenting vessels also will normally be larger—or more numerous. A small wooden cask, once cleaned, is satisfactory but the few casks available can be very expensive. Polythene vessels, holding up to 5 gallons, with a tap at the bottom, are more easily obtainable and easier to clean.

A nylon sieve is necessary for straining and a large plastic funnel for filling the jars.

A rack is useful for storing filled bottles, if corks are used. The rack holds the bottle at an angle so that the cork is always in contact with the wine—if this is not done, the cork will dry out, become loose and no

A home wine-maker's work bench (right)

16

longer seal off the wine. If you use plastic stoppers, instead of corks, a rack is unnecessary as the bottles can be stood upright.

One or two plastic buckets will come in handy; obtain the sort marked on the inside with gallons and sub-divisions.

Optional Equipment

If you want to drink wine soon after the fermentation has finished, or if your wine does not clear, you will need filtering equipment. There are some excellent filters available which operate on the syphonage principle and do not require any attention while filtering is in progress. Other filters can be made with a nylon filter bag (2 gallon size—a support frame is also required), a plastic funnel plugged firmly with cotton wool and containing some cellulose pulp, refined diatomaceous silica or similar filteration agent. There are also a number of 'fining' (clearing) materials available; these are described later.

A hydrometer, reading from 0·990 to 1·170, with a trial jar enables the sugar content and the potential alcoholic strength of the wine to be accurately determined. A Vinometer is useful to measure the alcoholic content of the finished wine.

Racks for storing bottles at an angle

Safety bungs and corks are very useful. These are stoppers that seal the jar or bottle but allow any late, or secondary, fermentation gases to pass out instead of building up pressure inside the vessel, thus either forcing out the cork or even causing a burst.

Corks, capsules and self-adhesive labels are available in great variety. Nylon brushes for cleaning out jars are very necessary—they can be obtained with handles of various lengths to suit the depth of the vessel. Bottles are more easily cleaned with a length of chromed chain as used for bath or sink plugs. Drop the chain in the bottle and swirl it round and round and to and fro with a little hot water.

18

A combined plastic pump and syphon provides the easiest method of filling the bottles from the fermenting jar.

Self-adhesive labels are useful for labelling jars or bottles before storage—it is easy to forget their contents after a few weeks. Write on the labels the quantities of all the ingredients, the date fermentation commenced, the date when put into store and other relevant information. If you copy these labels into a book you will have a complete record of your wine making activities and an opportunity to repeat or amend a recipe on a subsequent occasion.

Hygiene

Cleanliness is of the greatest importance, but fortunately it is not difficult to make up a sterilizing solution. Sterilized vessels should be kept covered to guard against airborne bacteria and the vinegar fly, which can turn your wine into vinegar.

A few ounces of sodium metabilsulphite is easy to obtain, or crushed Campden tablets will serve the same purpose; when dissolved, they produce sulphur dioxide. It is convenient to make up a stock solution in a pint bottle—use about $\frac{1}{2}$ oz. of sodium metabisulphite or 7 or 8 Campden tablets dissolved in warm water. Half a teaspoon of citric acid adds to its potency. Do not inhale the fumes, and keep the stock solution well corked.

To sterilize, pour a small quantity into one of the bottles, swirl it around then tip it into the next, and so on. The same method applies to the larger vessels. When the solution has lost its characteristic smell, throw it away. If there are any deposits on the vessels, remove them by brush or loose chain, as already described. After this has been done, empty the vessels if you are going to use them immediately, but do not rinse them in water; just cover them securely. There is no harm in leaving a little of the solution in each vessel before putting them aside for later use.

Corks, bungs, fermentation traps and your pump-syphon should all be soaked or rinsed through with the solution before use.

If you happen to acquire a wooden cask, make sure that it is fully swelled and thoroughly cleaned. First, fill it completely with cold water and leave it for several hours, then scald it with boiling water to which lime has been added. If you have a long brush use it as far as it will reach around the inside. Then empty the cask and have a good sniff at the bung hole—if there is any musty or unpleasant smell, scald it again. Finally, rinse it out well with a gallon of so of your sterilizing solution. A filled cask must be kept in a dry, airy place. If the atmosphere is damp or humid the wine will evaporate and it is the alcohol that evaporates first.

Fermentation lock with cork (above left)
Barrels for storing wine during
fermentation (above right)
Selection of corks and stoppers (right)

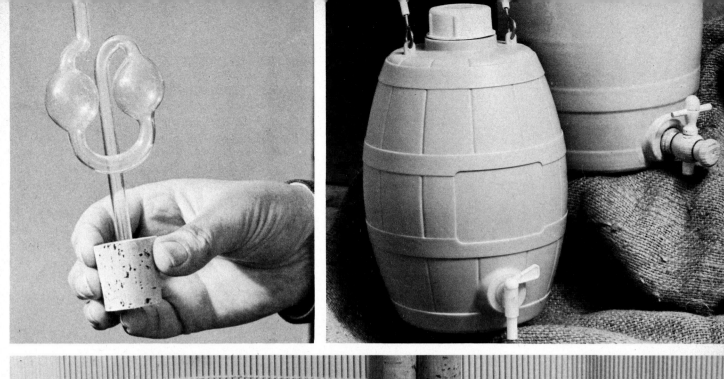

Basic techniques

If you decide to use only concentrated juice extracts for your wine, the next heading that will concern you is Fermentation. Concentrated cans of grape and other fruit juices always carry full instructions for making up the must before adding the yeast, and until some experience has been gained it is best to follow these instructions. When you feel like experimenting more, it is good practice to measure the specific gravity (S.G.) of the extract before adding sugar, as described below.

Making the Must

The must is the extract of juice before fermentation. Extraction is performed by boiling, crushing, or soaking, the method depending on the raw material—details of the preparation required are given with each recipe.

Boiling—the wash boiler or large pan is required for some fruit and the harder vegetable roots, but it must not be done for too long, or the flavour will be lost. The liquor is finally strained and cooled. A pressure cooker is much quicker but rather tedious if larger quantities are involved.

Soaking in hot water—boiling water is poured over the ingredients which are left to soak for three or four days —this method applies especially to dried fruits and berries. Sometimes they must be boiled up first.

Soaking in cold water—soaking may be required for several days to reduce the fruit to a pulpy state. The pulp must then be strained to remove most of the solids.

Pressing—this method is suitable for soft fruits such as grapes, blackberries, raspberries or bilberries.

Electric Slicers, Liquidizers or Extractors—most fruit and vegetables can be put through the liquidizer—the juices of soft fruits can be strained and are ready for use, but the pulp of root vegetables will still require boiling.

The must now needs to be strained—if it is new, rinse out your nylon filter bag in hot water then set it up with a plastic bucket below, and pour the pulp into the bag. The liquid will have filtered through in 6 or 12 hours.

It often helps if canned grape juice is added to fruit or vegetable musts, or alternatively, chopped raisins or sultanas add 'a body'.

Wine made from most ingredients will taste rather flat unless citric or tartaric acid and tannin are included. The exact quantities depend on individual taste. Citric acid dissolves easily, but first mix the tannin into a paste with a little water, as otherwise it is inclined to form a sticky lump. The pectin-destroying enzyme is added to the must at an early stage. It is assumed that you are going to make 4 gallons of wine and have a 5 gallon fermentation jar, with tap.

Now test the specific gravity of the must with a hydrometer. All the fruit or vegetable ingredients likely to be used for wine making contain some sugar, and the

Straining the must (right)

20

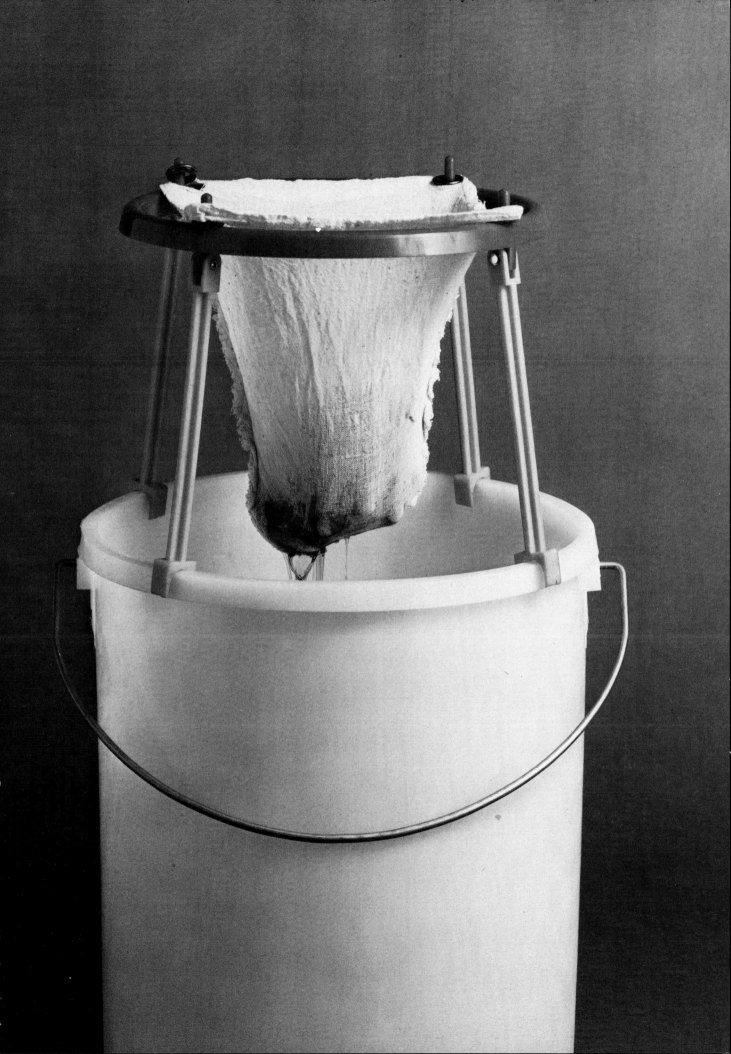

object is to measure the amount of sugar present so as to be able to calculate how much more to add. Top up the must with cold water to a definite volume (for this reason it is best to use plastic buckets calibrated on the inside. You have to know the volume in order to translate the hydrometer readings into ounces of sugar).

If you do not want to bother with the hydrometer and specific gravities, just add the sugar shown with each recipe. These are average quantities and although they may be too small to produce the full alcohol potential, or too large to convert fully into alcohol, so that the finished wine is too sweet, nevertheless they will produce wine that you are almost certain to enjoy.

Refer to the specific gravity curve and read off the number of ounces of sugar in the gallon corresponding to the hydrometer reading, and multiply by the number of gallons you have in the bucket to get the total weight of sugar present. Thus if the hydrometer reading is 1·030, the amount of sugar present is $9\frac{1}{2}$ ounces, and as you have (say) $1\frac{1}{2}$ gallons of liquid, the total weight of sugar is $9\frac{1}{2}$ times 1·5 equals 14·25 ounces, say 14. Now decide what you want the S.G. of the completed must to be, when it is made up to 4 gallons. Generally speaking, an S.G. of 1·080 will give a dry wine, 1·100 a demi-sec, and 1·120 a sweet wine. 1·085 is a good figure to aim at.

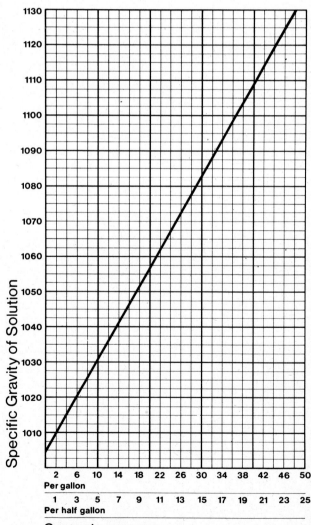

Sugar in ounces

Adding the Sugar

Refer again to the graph. An S.G. of 1·085 ought to be obtained by having 31 oz. to the gallon, and as you are going to have 4 gallons of must when it is ready for the yeast, the sugar required is 31 times 4 equals 124 oz. You already have 14 oz. in the must, so it appears that 110 oz. more, or 6 lb. 14 oz., is required.

You now require a 5-gallon, calibrated container. A very convenient container is a 5-gallon plastic jar with a tap at the bottom (the tap is important). It will not be calibrated when bought, but calibration is easily effected by using a gallon measure (for instance, one of the plastic buckets). Fill the jar a gallon at a time and mark the water surface (which can be seen through the side) at each gallon. A felt pen makes a satisfactory marker. While the must is still in the bucket, add 4 lb. sugar and stir until it dissolves, which it will do at room temperature; pour the mixture into a plastic jar. Dissolve another 2 lb. sugar in another gallon of water, and add that; you now have 3 gallons of diluted must in the jar, you have added 6 lb. sugar, and there was 14 oz. natural sugar to start with. Shake the jar (not too difficult, though it now weighs 30 lb.) and draw off a sample (in a milk bottle, for instance) from the tap.

Test the S.G. again, and recalculate the total amount of sugar in the must from the curve, multiplying by 3 now, because you have 3 gallons in the jar. You will probably find that the quantity does not come out exactly as you thought, but your estimate is more accurate now as you are dealing with larger quantities.

Suppose the new S.G. is 1·090. The curve tells you that you have 33 oz. to the gallon, and the total amount is therefore 33 times 3 or 99 oz. (which includes the 14 oz. in the original extract). You need another 25 oz., or 1 lb. 9 oz. Weigh this out, and dissolve it in another gallon of water in a bucket, and pour it into the jar (do not forget to put your sample back). Shake it up if you can, or stir it, and draw another sample for another S.G. reading. It should be 1·085. Do not worry if it is not quite correct; it will be near enough.

Of course, sugar dissolves most easily in hot water, but the reason for using cold water is that with hot water the temperature of the must will be raised a great deal and you will either have to apply a temperature correction to the hydrometer reading, or wait until the lot has cooled down, as the temperature affects the S.G. reading obtained. Temperature corrections are given on the sheet which comes with the hydrometer, but then you need a thermometer as well.

Many wine makers advocate the addition of the sugar in stages, say half with the yeast or initial fermentation, and the second half 10 or 14 days later, perhaps when you strain off the juice from the initial fermentation.

Home wine making is not an exact science—two similar brews can turn out quite differently. Do not be discouraged if your first effort is disappointing—there is

Grapes for making wine (top left)
Wash berries well before use (centre left)
Preparing the must (left)
Adding sugar to the must (below)

nearly always some other amateur who will be only too
pleased to help with difficulties.

Fermentation

Now you are ready to add the yeast. The reason for
choosing a plastic jar for mixing up the brew is so that
the jar can be used as a fermenting vessel. One could
alternatively decant the brew into four separate glass
1-gallon containers, which are easier for fitting the
fermentation traps. Plastic traps break less easily. If
you are only making one gallon, there is no problem.
There are dozens of different types of yeasts, all bearing
full instructions. Some are ready-mixed with yeast
energizer, although with canned grape juice concentrate
an energizer is not usually required.

The must should be raised to a temperature of 70°F
(21°C) before adding the yeast—with the canned concentrates this is achieved by diluting with warm water.
With some yeasts a starter bottle is recommended. This
means taking a pint bottle, adding the yeast, the
energizer, 2 oz. sugar and perhaps the juice of an
orange; fill the bottle three-quarters full with warm
water, plug the top with cotton wool and stand it in a
warm place. It is easy to see when fermentation really
gets going; froth and bubbles will pile up inside the
bottle, when it can be emptied into the warm must.

Alternatively, the dried, granular yeasts—about half an
ounce, or as directed on the sachet—can be added
directly to the must. Some recipes, especially those
containing a large proportion of vegetable matter to
juice, benefit if the initial fermentation takes place in a
vessel not completely closed to air ('aerobic fermentation') either with cloth(s) covering a wide vessel, or with
a cotton wool plug in the bung hole. During the aerobic
fermentation period, stir the fermenting liquid every day
or two. After 10 to 14 days, strain off the liquid into a
vessel that can be sealed by a fermentation trap.

This trap, which is partly filled with water, allows carbon
dioxide gas to escape, but keeps out airborne bacteria.
This is known as the 'anerobic fermentation' period.
When the trap is fitted the temperature can be reduced
to 65°F (18°C).

The must is left alone for four or five weeks until all
bubbles cease—in warm weather they will often start up
again after a day or two, so do not be in too much of a
hurry. When you think it is done, draw off a sample
from the tap or by your syphon-pump and test the S.G.
If it is below 1·005 it is done, but S.G. 1·000 is better
(i.e. more sugar has been converted into alcohol); ·990
is better still—a very dry wine—with the maximum
alcoholic strength obtainable from the quantity of
sugar in, or added to, the must. If the wine is too dry to
the taste, sugar can now be added without destroying
the alcoholic strength attained.

Adding yeast to the must (above left)
Straining the liquid after the initial
fermentation (above centre)
Filling the fermentation trap (above right)
Partially filling the trap with water (right)

24

Racking, Filtering, Clearing and Storage

There is nothing to stop you filtering the wine—and drinking it—immediately. Filtering is necessary because the wine will still be cloudy, but it is better to let it mature and clear naturally. So, you must first rack it—that is to say, syphon off the wine from the dead yeast and other material (the 'lees') in the bottom of the fermentation vessel, into clean containers. Add two crushed Campden tablets per gallon while you are doing this in order to kill off any bacteria. Throw away the lees and top up your new vessels nearly full with either another similar, clear wine or cooled boiled water. This prevents oxidation.

Label all the jars, then store the wine in a dark place at a temperature of around 50°F (10°C) for as long as you can; rack it off every six to eight weeks or whenever a quantity of lees form. Lees can impart 'off' flavours to the wine if left.

Canned grape concentrates will often clear completely in six weeks or two months, but some fruit or vegetable wines need a year or more although they can always be filtered clear and drunk before then. In general, however, the longer the wines are left, the better the flavour. This waiting period is known as maturation, that is, the wine is maturing.

There are other clearing or 'fining' methods besides filtration—white of egg, well beaten and added to a little wine; Bentonite, a very finely divided clay; isinglass and various proprietary finings. All of these are stirred int to the cloudy wine and during the next week or two will slowly sink to the bottom, carrying the unwanted particles with them.

For filtering, there are the proprietary filters which include full instructions; you can use diatomaceous silica —a very fine powder that is mixed with the wine and allowed to drip through your nylon bag—but this operation usually has to be repeated a few times for full clarification of the wine.

Another method is to plug a funnel with cotton wool, sprinkle in a half-inch layer of cellulose powder and allow the wine to drip through into a jug. When the jug is about half full the powder will have started to settle in the bottom of the funnel, which can now be transferred to a support over a pail or other receptacle. When refilling the funnel, pour the wine gently down the side of the funnel, as far as possible, so as to disturb the wad of cellulose powder as little as possible. Pour back into the funnel the half filled jug of wine, since the filter was not at full effectiveness until the powder had settled.

Asbestos powder is also available instead of cellulose powder, but asbestos is not in great favour today because it is a possible health risk.

Of all fining methods, Bentonite is probably the easiest to use and gives the most spectacular results; some hazes will not clear entirely even after two or three passes through filters, but one application of Bentonite is almost guaranteed to produce a really bright wine. The method of using it is as follows.

Pour nearly a pint of boiled, cooled water into a clean, screw-topped glass or plastic bottle. Add 2 oz. of Bentonite powder, screw on the top and shake vigorously. Let the bottle stand for half an hour, then shake vigorously again. Repeat this agitation, say, 5 or 6 times, when nearly all the Bentonite will go into suspension (that is, there will be scarcely any sediment after the bottle has stood for a couple of hours). Now let the bottle stand for 24 hours; during this time the Bentonite particles will swell.

When ready to add to the wine, which should have been recently racked, shake up the Bentonite once more and prepare to add two or three tablespoons of the Bentonite solution per gallon. If the wine container is really full, pour off a little of the wine first, to make room for the Bentonite.

Close the wine container, then agitate it by stirring or swirling to mix the Bentonite thoroughly. Repeat this agitation once or twice during the next half hour. Then let the Bentonite settle for a week. The wine should be perfectly clear after this time. Exact measurements and dosage rates are not important—if the wine is very cloudy add rather more of the solution.

Decanting and Serving

When you want to use the wine, you will need six wine bottles per gallon—use clear bottles for white or rosé wines, and dark green or brown for red wines—this helps to preserve the bright red colour.

If the wine is not going to be stored use flanged corks or plastic stoppers as no corkscrew is required to remove them. On the other hand, for storage, use long corks, after soaking them in sterilizing solution to kill off any bacteria. A 'flogger' will drive the corks home—a 'flogger' is merely a fairly heavy chunk of wood with a handle; more elaborate corking tools are available.

Syphon the wine out of the storage vessel, being careful not to disturb any sediment. If the bottles are kept for some while before drinking, pour carefully, as the bottle is emptied, as more sediment is likely to form. If the red wine tastes harsh, add glycerine at the rate of 2 oz. per gallon.

White wine is usually chilled before serving—not too cold—about an hour in the refrigerator is adequate. Red wine, on the other hand, is served at room temperature; it is beneficial to uncork a bottle of red wine an hour or so before it is to be used.

Bowl shaped glasses hold the bouquet of the wine; do not fill the glasses more than two-thirds full.

If you have produced a wine that is too sweet, or too dry, blending with another wine of opposite character will result in a finished product more to your taste.

Racking the wine (above left)

Trimming corks with a sharp knife (above right)

Corks may be covered with foil caps (left)

Wine recipes

Reminders

As we have said, wine making is not an exact science and every recipe given in this book can be changed to suit individual taste.

In general it is beneficial to the body of the wine to add red or white canned grape juice concentrate to most non-grape wines. Conversely, it is beneficial to many red wines to add juice from dark berries such as elderberries, blackberries, blackcurrants or bilberries. Red wines are usually more satisfactory and easier to make. Grape wines are usually self-sufficient in tannin and citric acid, but nearly all other wines benefit from their addition—for suggested quantities see the next section. The quantity of sugar to be added to each recipe should be sufficient to raise the starting S.G. to 1·085, as explained on page 22, if you are using a hydrometer. If not, follow the recipe quantity which should give satisfactory results.

The yeast added can either be fermented in a starter bottle, or added direct to the must, in both cases with yeast nutrient as explained on page 24.

To all fruit (except grape concentrates) and vegetable wines, it is beneficial to add a pectin destroying enzyme such as Pectinase, Pectozyme or Pectinol.

Fermentation and Storage

The word 'additives' in these recipes includes citric acid, grape tannin, pectin destroying enzyme and Campden tablets. The general quantities for these additives are

Yeast nutrient	1 teaspoon ($\frac{4}{5}$ teaspoon) per gallon of must
Citric Acid	1 teaspoon ($\frac{4}{5}$ teaspoon) per gallon of must
Grape Tannin	$\frac{1}{2}$ teaspoon ($\frac{2}{5}$ teaspoon) per gallon of must
Pectin destroying enzyme	As directed on label of bottle
Campden tablets	One, crushed, is required to be added to the must of some recipes.

These quantities can be adjusted to taste.

The words 'aerobic fermentation period' mean the period from adding the yeast, sugar, etc for initial fermentation with the fermenting vessel at a temperature of about 70°F (21°C), covered with cloth or plugged with cotton wool. During this period stir the mixture at least once daily and keep it about 70°F (21°C).

When the period indicated has elapsed, strain off the juice and put it into a clean vessel fitted with a fermentation trap. This is when the 'aerobic fermentation period' commences. Canned concentrated juices and certain other wines, as indicated in the recipes, do not benefit from an aerobic fermentation period and can be put into a closed vessel with fermentation trap straight

Serving your wine (right)

28

away. During the aerobic fermentation period, do not allow the temperature to fall below 60°F (15·5°C); 65°F (18°C) is better.

If the temperature does fall, no harm is likely to result, but fermentation will cease until the temperature is raised again. When all bubbling has ceased, and all froth on top of the wine has died away, fermentation is over. Rack the wine into a clean vessel and seal. Further rackings should take place as sediment forms, perhaps once every month or two months.

Apple Wine

If a dry table wine is preferred, reduce the sugar by half.

Main ingredients	**8 lb. apples (cookers are best)** **4 oz. (⅔ cup) barley** **4 oz. (1 cup) chopped sultanas**
Other ingredients	**yeast, yeast nutrient** **rind and juice of 1 lemon**
Water	**1 gallon (1⅓ gallon) water**
Sugar	**4 lb. demerara sugar**
Additives	**citric acid, pectin destroying** **enzyme** **2 Campden tablets**

Core the apples and discard the pips. Chop the remainder into small pieces, put them into a large bowl, add the crushed Campden tablets (they will stop the apples browning), and the barley, sultanas, water and the rind and juice of the lemon. Stir and press the mixture every day for three weeks.

Strain into another bowl already containing the sugar, then stir until the sugar dissolves. Add the yeast, nutrient and other additives, then follow the general instructions for fermentation and storage.

Aerobic fermentation period
(without fermentation trap): 3 weeks

Anaerobic fermentation period
(with fermentation trap): 6 weeks

Colour: White

Classification: Dessert

Minimum storage period: 6 months

Fermentation and storage
During the aerobic fermentation period, stir the fermenting material at least once daily, and keep it at 70°F (21°C). When the period indicated has elapsed, strain off the juice and put it into a clean vessel fitted with a fermentation trap.

During the anaerobic fermentation period, maintain the temperature above 60°F (15.5°C). When bubbling ceases and the froth dies away, rack the wine into a clean, sealed vessel.

Apple and orange wine
30

Apple and Bilberry Wine

Main ingredients	6 lb. apples—cooking apples are best
	4 lb. bilberries
	½ lb. raisins or sultanas
Other ingredients	yeast, yeast nutrient
Water	1 gallon (1⅕ gallon) water
Sugar	3½ lb. white sugar
Additives	citric acid, pectin destroying enzyme

Chop the apples, rejecting bruised parts, but do not peel. Discard the pips, which make the wine bitter. Put them in a bowl with half the water; stir and press them for a week, then strain.

Three days after you have put the apples in the water, cover the bilberries with the rest of the water, leave for 4 days, then squeeze well and strain.

Combine the liquids from the two fruits.

Add the chopped raisins and sugar to the liquid and stir until sugar dissolves. Add yeast, then follow the general instructions for fermentation and storage.

Aerobic fermentation period (without fermentation trap): 3 weeks

Anaerobic fermentation period (with fermentation trap): 6 weeks

Colour: Dark

Classification: Dessert

Minimum storage period: 6 months

Fermentation and storage:
During the aerobic fermentation period, stir the fermenting material at least once daily, and keep it at 70°F (21°C). When the period indicated has elapsed, strain off the juice and put it into a clean vessel fitted with a fermentation trap.

During the anaerobic fermentation period, maintain the temperature above 60°F (15·5°C). When bubbling ceases and the froth dies away, rack the wine into a clean, sealed vessel.

Apple and Orange Wine

Main ingredients	6 lb. Bramley ápples
	6 large oranges
Other ingredients	yeast, yeast nutrient
Water	1 gallon (1⅕ gallon) water
Sugar	4 lb. white sugar
Additives	citric acid, pectin destroying enzyme

Cut the apples into small pieces, after coring. Discard pips. Peel off the orange skins in four sections, removing loose pith. Add the skins, with the sliced orange, to the apples. Pour over boiling water and when tepid, add the yeast, nutrient, additives and the sugar. Then follow the general instructions for fermentation and storage.

Aerobic fermentation period (without fermentation trap): 4 days, then remove the orange skins, but avoid squeezing them or the wine will be bitter. Strain as usual

Anaerobic fermentation period (with fermentation trap): 4 weeks

Colour: Golden

Classification: Dessert

Minimum storage period: 6 months

Fermentation and storage:
During the aerobic fermentation period, stir the fermenting material at least once daily, and keep it at 70°F (21°C). When the period indicated has elapsed, strain off the juice and put it into a clean vessel fitted with a fermentation trap.

During the anaerobic fermentation period, maintain the temperature above 60°F (15·5°C). When bubbling ceases and the froth dies away, rack the wine into a clean, sealed vessel.

Fresh Apricot Wine

If fresh apricots are not available try the recipe for Apricot wine on page 61 which uses dried apricots.

Main ingredient	4 lb. apricots
Other ingredients	yeast, yeast nutrient
Water	1 gallon (1⅕ gallon) water
Sugar	3 lb. white sugar
Additives	citric acid, grape tannin, pectin destroying enzyme

Stone the apricots; crack a dozen or so of the stones and put the kernels with the fruit. Boil the apricots and kernels together in the water until the apricots are tender; strain the liquid off on to the sugar. (The apricots can be used in desserts.)

When the liquid has cooled, add the yeast, nutrient and additives, then follow the general instructions for fermentation and storage.

(recipe continued overleaf)

Preparing fresh apples for apple wine

**Aerobic fermentation period
(without fermentation trap):** 2 days

**Anaerobic fermentation period
(with fermentation trap):** 3–4 weeks

Colour: Golden

Classification: Table

Minimum storage period: 6 to 9 months

Fermentation and storage:
During the aerobic fermentation period, stir the fermenting material at least once daily, and keep it at 70°F (21°C). When the period indicated has elapsed, strain off the juice and put it into a clean vessel fitted with a fermentation trap. During the anaerobic fermentation period, maintain the temperature above 60°F (15·5°C). When bubbling ceases and the froth dies away, rack the wine into a clean, sealed vessel.

Banana Wine

A few old bananas can be added to many fruit wines with good results. Dried bananas can also be used in this recipe. An ounce each of cloves and ginger will make a delicious spiced wine.

Main ingredients	**4 lb. peeled bananas (old ones are best)** **½ lb. banana skins** **¼ lb. chopped raisins**
Other ingredients	**juice of 1 lemon** **juice of 1 orange** **yeast, yeast nutrient**
Water	**1 gallon (1⅕ gallon) water**
Sugar	**3 lb. white sugar**
Additives	**citric acid, grape tannin, pectin destroying enzyme**

Place bananas and skins in a muslin bag, tie up into boiler or pan, add water, boil and let simmer for ½ hour. Pour the hot juice over the sugar, orange and lemon juice, and when cool, squeeze as much out of the bag as possible. Add the yeast, then follow the general instructions for fermentation and storage.

**Aerobic fermentation period
(without fermentation trap):** 7 days. Siphon off juice and add raisins, then fit airlock

**Anaerobic fermentation period
(with fermentation trap):** 4 months

Colour: White

Classification: Dessert

Minimum storage period: 6 months–1 year

Fermentation and storage:
During the aerobic fermentation period, stir the fermenting material at least once daily, and keep it at 70°F (21°C). When the period indicated has elapsed, strain off the juice and put it into a clean vessel fitted with a fermentation trap. During the anaerobic fermentation period, maintain the temperature above 60°F (15·5°C). When bubbling ceases and the froth dies away, rack the wine into a clean, sealed vessel.

Fresh Bilberry Wine

Fresh bilberries can be hard to come by, but dried berries obtainable at most home wine suppliers are an excellent substitute, and make a wine with an unusual flavour, subtle and intriguing. In Scotland, bilberries are known as blaeberries and in the United States, of course, as blueberries.

Main ingredient	**2 lb. fresh bilberries**
Other ingredients	**yeast, yeast nutrient**
Water	**3 quart (3¾ quart) water**
Sugar	**2 lb. white sugar**
Additives	**citric acid, pectin destroying enzyme**

Wash the berries, put into fermentation bowl and pour half the boiling water over them. Stir in the sugar and citric acid, then add the remaining water. When this liquid has become lukewarm, add the other ingredients and additives, then follow the general instructions for fermentation and storage.

**Aerobic fermentation period
(without fermentation trap):** 4–5 days

**Anaerobic fermentation period
(with fermentation trap):** 4–5 months

Colour: Red

Classification: Table

Minimum storage period: 6 months

Fermentation and storage:
During the aerobic fermentation period, stir the fermenting material at least once daily, and keep it at 70°F (21°C). When the period indicated has elapsed, strain off the juice and put it into a clean vessel fitted with a fermentation trap. During the anaerobic fermentation period, maintain the temperature above 60°F (15·5°C). When bubbling ceases and the froth dies away, rack the wine into a clean, sealed vessel.

Blackberry Wine

This wine benefits from the addition of ¼ lb. of canned red grape juice concentrate.

Main ingredient	**4 lb. blackberries**
Other ingredients	**yeast, yeast nutrient** **juice and rind of 1 lemon**
Water	**1 gallon (1⅕ gallon) water**
Sugar	**3 lb. brown sugar**
Additives	**citric acid, grape tannin, pectin** **destroying enzyme** **1 Campden tablet**

Wash the berries gently in cold water containing one crushed Campden tablet. Put the berries, lemon juice and rind in a large bowl. Pour boiling water over them and leave to stand three days, stirring daily. Strain through a muslin or nylon bag on to the sugar and stir well. Mix the yeast with a little liquid and add to the mixture, then follow the general instructions for fermentation and storage.

Aerobic fermentation period
 (without fermentation-trap): 2 days

Anaerobic fermentation period
 (with fermentation trap): 4–6 weeks

Colour: Red

Classification: Dessert

Minimum storage period: 6–9 months

Fermentation and storage:

During the aerobic fermentation period, stir the fermenting material at least once daily, and keep it at 70°F (21°C). When the period indicated has elapsed, strain off the juice and put it into a clean vessel fitted with a fermentation trap.

During the anaerobic fermentation period, maintain the temperature above 60°F (15·5°C). When bubbling ceases and the froth dies away, rack the wine into a clean, sealed vessel.

Grapes from the Bordeaux region

Wine is most easily made from grapes (left)
Home-made wine in fermentation jars (below)
Using home-made wines in cooking (right)

Blackberry and Elderberry Wine

The fruits in this wine may be added to, so long as you keep the required amount of sugar. You could substitute sloes and rowanberries for some of the blackberries and elderberries.

Main ingredients	**2 lb. blackberries**
	2 lb. elderberries
Other ingredients	**yeast, yeast nutrient**
Water	**1 gallon (1⅕ gallon) water**
Sugar	**3 lb. white sugar**
Additives	**citric acid, pectin destroying enzyme**

Wash and dry the fruit carefully. Wild berries are more likely to have maggots or small flies on them, so after washing them it is a good precaution to soak them for a while in water in which a Campden tablet has been dissolved. Use enough water to cover. Then throw this water away and rinse the berries again.

Place the berries in a large basin or wooden bowl and crush them with a wooden spoon. Pour the boiling water over them and stir well. Strain through a nylon bag or nylon sieve on to the sugar and stir well until the sugar is dissolved. Add the yeast, nutrient and additives, then follow the general instructions for fermentation and storage.

**Aerobic fermentation period
(without fermentation trap):** 4 days

**Anaerobic fermentation period
(with fermentation trap):** 4–6 weeks

Colour: Red

Classification: Dessert

Minimum storage period: 6 months

Fermentation and storage:
During the aerobic fermentation period, stir the fermenting material at least once daily, and keep it at 70°F (21°C). When the period indicated has elapsed, strain off the juice and put it into a clean vessel fitted with a fermentation trap.

During the anaerobic fermentation period, maintain the temperature above 60°F (15·5°C). When bubbling ceases and the froth dies away, rack the wine into a clean, sealed vessel.

A selection of berries for making wines (right)

A selection of vegetables for making wine (right)

A home wine-maker's work bench (below)

Ginger Blackberry Wine

Main ingredient	2 lb. blackberries
Other ingredients	yeast, yeast nutrient ½ oz. essence of ginger
Water	1 gallon (1⅕ gallon) water
Sugar	4 lb. white sugar
Additives	grape tannin, pectin destroying enzyme ½ oz. tartaric acid

Put the berries into the boiling water for ten minutes or longer, then strain and squeeze all the moisture from the fruit before throwing the pulp away. Add the sugar, tartaric acid, yeast and additives, then follow the general instructions for fermentation and storage.

Aerobic fermentation period
(without fermentation trap): 18 days then add the ginger

Anaerobic fermentation period
(with fermentation trap): 2 weeks

Colour: Red

Classification: Dessert

Minimum storage period: 6 months or more

Fermentation and storage:
During the aerobic fermentation period, stir the fermenting material at least once daily, and keep it at 70°F (21°C). When the period indicated has elapsed, strain off the juice and put it into a clean vessel fitted with a fermentation trap.
During the anaerobic fermentation period, maintain the temperature above 60°F (15·5°C). When bubbling ceases and the froth dies away, rack the wine into a clean, sealed vessel.

Blackcurrant Wine (1)

Main ingredient	1 gallon (1⅕ gallon) blackcurrants
Other ingredients	yeast, yeast nutrient
Water	1 gallon (1⅕ gallon) water
Sugar	3½ lb. white sugar
Additives	citric acid, pectin destroying enzyme

Put the currants and the water together and bring to the boil slowly, simmering until all the goodness is in the water (about 20 minutes). Then strain.
Put the sugar into a bowl. Pour over the boiling blackcurrant liquid and stir until the sugar is dissolved.
When lukewarm, add the yeast, nutrient and additives then follow the general instructions for fermentation and storage.

**Aerobic fermentation period
(without fermentation trap):** 14 days

**Anaerobic fermentation period
(with fermentation trap):** 4–6 weeks

Colour: Red

Classification: Dessert

Minimum storage period: 1 to 2 years

Fermentation and storage:
During the aerobic fermentation period, stir the fermenting material at least once daily, and keep it at 70°F (21°C). When the period indicated has elapsed, strain off the juice and put it into a clean vessel fitted with a fermentation trap. During the anaerobic fermentation period, maintain the temperature above 60°F (15·5°C). When bubbling ceases and the froth dies away, rack the wine into a clean, sealed vessel.

Blackcurrant Wine (2)

Main ingredient	**12 oz. bottle of Ribena (blackcurrant) syrup**
Other ingredients	**yeast, yeast nutrient**
Water	**1 gallon (1⅕ gallon) water**
Sugar	**2½ lb. white sugar**
Additive	**citric acid**

Dissolve the sugar in hot water then add this syrup to all the other ingredients in the fermenting jar and fill up with warm water. Stir well, then follow the general instructions for fermentation and storage.

**Aerobic fermentation period
(without fermentation trap):** 1 week

**Anaerobic fermentation period
(with fermentation trap):** 4 weeks

Colour: Red

Classification: Dessert

Minimum storage period: 2 months

Fermentation and storage:
During the aerobic fermentation period, stir the fermenting material at least once daily, and keep it at 70°F (21°C). When the period indicated has elapsed, strain off the juice and put it into a clean vessel fitted with a fermentation trap.
During the anaerobic fermentation period, maintain the temperature above 60°F (15·5°C). When bubbling ceases and the froth dies away, rack the wine into a clean, sealed vessel.

illustrations on pages 44 and 45:
Fruit and vegetables for home-made wines (left)
Orange wine (right)

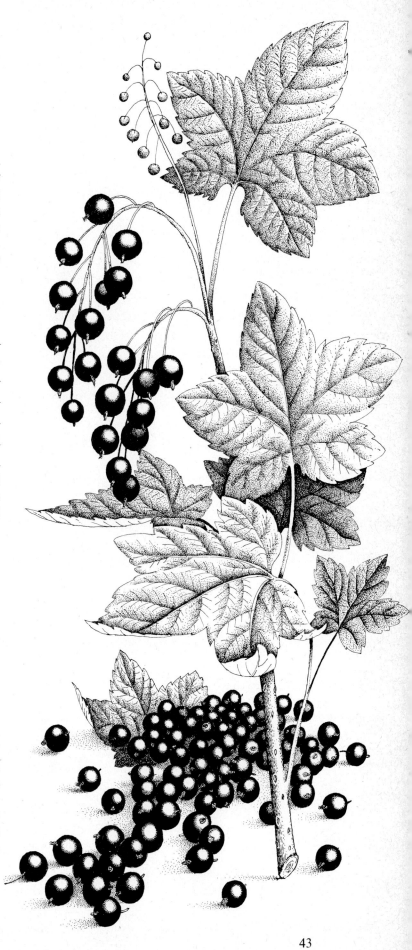

Cherry Wine

Main ingredient	8 lb. Morello cherries
Other ingredients	yeast, yeast nutrient
Water	1 gallon (1⅕ gallon) water
Sugar	3½ lb. white sugar
Additives	citric acid, pectin destroying enzyme 1 Campden tablet

Place the washed fruit in a bowl with all of the water, add the yeast, nutrient and all the additives, crushing the Campden tablet. Keep covered for 10 days, gradually crushing the cherries. Then strain off the liquor into the fermentation vessel (allow plenty of time for this). Dissolve the sugar in hot water and add to the juice, then follow the general instructions for fermentation and storage.

Aerobic fermentation period (without fermentation trap): 4 days

Anaerobic fermentation period (with fermentation trap): 4–5 weeks

Colour: Red

Classification: Dessert

Minimum storage period: 6 months

Fermentation and storage:
During the aerobic fermentation period, stir the fermenting material at least once daily, and keep it at 70°F (21°C). When the period indicated has elapsed, strain off the juice and put it into a clean vessel fitted with a fermentation trap.
During the anaerobic fermentation period, maintain the temperature above 60°F (15·5°C). When bubbling ceases and the froth dies away, rack the wine into a clean, sealed vessel.

Cherry and Rhubarb Wine

Main ingredients	1 gallon (1⅕ gallon) of rhubarb, cut up with skin left on 3 lb. ripe red cherries, stoned ½ lb. chopped raisins ½ lb. wheat
Other ingredients	yeast, yeast nutrient
Water	1 gallon (1⅕ gallon) water
Sugar	4 lb. white sugar
Additives	citric acid, grape tannin, pectin destroying enzyme

Cover the rhubarb with a gallon (1⅕ gallon) of boiling water. Stand for eight to nine days, stirring daily and pressing the rhubarb against the sides of the bowl. Keep the bowl well covered. Strain, press all the moisture from the rhubarb and throw away the pulp.
Add the sugar, stoned cherries, raisins and wheat. Stir all this with your hand or with a wooden spoon to dissolve the sugar and squeeze the raisins and cherries. Add the yeast, nutrient and additives. Stir well, then follow the general instructions for fermentation and storage.

Aerobic fermentation period (without fermentation trap): 1 week

Anaerobic fermentation period (with fermentation trap): 4 weeks

Colour: Rosé

Classification: Table

Minimum storage period: 6 months

Fermentation and storage:
During the aerobic fermentation period, stir the fer-

menting material at least once daily, and keep it at 70°F (21°C). When the period indicated has elapsed, strain off the juice and put it into a clean vessel fitted with a fermentation trap.

During the anaerobic fermentation period, maintain the temperature above 60°F (15·5°C). When bubbling ceases and the froth dies away, rack the wine into a clean, sealed vessel.

Cherry Port Wine

Main ingredient	6 lb. black cherries, stoned
Other ingredients	yeast, yeast nutrient
Water	1 gallon (1⅕ gallon) water
Sugar	3 lb. demerara sugar
Additives	citric acid, grape tannin, pectin destroying enzyme

Crush the cherries in a large bowl until the juice runs freely. Pour the boiling water over them, and leave them to soak for two days; then strain through a nylon bag. Bring this strained juice to boiling point and pour it over the sugar and citric acid. Stir until the sugar is dissolved, then stir in the yeast, nutrient and additives, then follow the general instructions for fermentation and storage.

Aerobic fermentation period
(without fermentation trap): 14 days

Anaerobic fermentation period
(with fermentation trap): 2–3 months

Colour: Red

Classification: Dessert

Minimum storage period: 6–8 months

Fermentation and storage:
During the aerobic fermentation period, stir the fermenting material at least once daily, and keep it at 70°F (21°C). When the period indicated has elapsed, strain off the juice and put it into a clean vessel with a trap. During the anaerobic fermentation period, maintain the temperature above 60°F (15·5°C). When bubbling ceases and the froth dies away, rack the wine into a clean, sealed vessel.

Making cherry and rhubarb wine

Cranberry Wine

Main ingredients	1 gallon (1⅕ gallon) cranberries
	1½ tablespoons (2T) orange juice or liquid honey
	2 lb. chopped raisins
Other ingredients	yeast, yeast nutrient
Water	1 gallon (1⅕ gallon) water
Sugar	3 lb. white sugar
Additives	citric acid, pectin destroying enzyme

Boil the water and pour it over the cranberries. Press them daily with the hands or with a heavy wooden spoon. After six days, strain, squeezing all the moisture from the fruit. Throw the pulp away—or put it on your garden compost heap—and cover the liquid.
Add the chopped raisins and sugar, stirring well to dissolve the sugar. Bring to the boil, then strain into a fermentation vessel. When lukewarm, add the yeast, nutrient and additives then follow the general instructions for fermentation and storage.

**Aerobic fermentation period
(without fermentation trap):** 14 days

**Anaerobic fermentation period
(with fermentation trap):** 2 weeks

Colour: Red

Classification: Dessert

Minimum storage period: 6 months

Fermentation and storage:
During the aerobic fermentation period, stir the fermenting material at least once daily, and keep it at 70°F (21°C). When the period indicated has elapsed, strain off the juice and put it into a clean vessel fitted with a fermentation trap.
During the anaerobic fermentation period, maintain the temperature above 60°F (15·5°C). When bubbling ceases and the froth dies away, rack the wine into a clean, sealed vessel.

Elderberry Wine

Main ingredients	4 lb. ripe elderberries
	½ lb. chopped raisins
Other ingredients	yeast, yeast nutrient
	rind and juice of 1 lemon
	1 piece bruised root ginger
Water	1 gallon (1⅕ gallon) water
Sugar	3 lb. white sugar
Additives	citric acid, pectin destroying enzyme

Grape wine

Strip the berries from the stalks. Boil in the water for 10 minutes. Strain, add the sugar, lemon juice, ginger and chopped raisins to the liquid and simmer for 20 minutes. Let the mixture cool in the bowl, then add the yeast, nutrient, and additives, then follow the general instructions for fermentation and storage.

**Aerobic fermentation period
(without fermentation trap):** 3 weeks

**Anaerobic fermentation period
(with fermentation trap):** 6 months

Colour: Red

Classification: Dessert

Minimum storage period: 3 months

Fermentation and storage:
During the aerobic fermentation period, stir the fermenting material at least once daily, and keep it at 70°F (21°C). When the period indicated has elapsed, strain off the juice and put it into a clean vessel fitted with a fermentation trap.
During the anaerobic fermentation period, maintain the temperature above 60°F (15·5°C). When bubbling ceases and the froth dies away, rack the wine into a clean, sealed vessel.

Elderberry and Malt Wine

Main ingredient	4 lb. elderberries
Other ingredients	yeast, yeast nutrient
	1 lb. malt extract
Water	1 gallon (1⅕ gallon) water
Sugar	3 lb. white sugar
Additives	citric acid, pectin destroying enzyme

Strip the berries from the stalks before weighing them, then crush well in a bowl. Add the malt extract and pour on the boiling water, stirring thoroughly. Cool to 70°F (21°C), add the yeast, nutrient and the additives. Then follow the general instructions for fermentation and storage.

**Aerobic fermentation period
(without fermentation trap):** 3 days

**Anaerobic fermentation period
(with fermentation trap):** 4 weeks

Colour: Red

Classification: Dessert

Minimum storage period: 6 months

Fermentation and storage:
During the aerobic fermentation period, stir the fer-

menting material at least once daily, and keep it at 70°F (21°C). When the period indicated has elapsed, strain off the juice and put it into a clean vessel with a trap. During the anaerobic fermentation period, maintain the temperature above 60°F (15·5°C). When bubbling ceases and the froth dies away, rack the wine into a clean, sealed vessel.

Elderberry Port

Main ingredients	1 gallon (1⅕ gallon) elderberries ½ lb. chopped raisins 1 lb. wheat
Other ingredients	yeast, yeast nutrient
Water	1 gallon (1⅕ gallon) water
Sugar	3 lb. white sugar
Additives	citric acid, pectin destroying enzyme

Strip the elderberries from the stalks. Place in boiling water and simmer for 15 minutes, then strain through a muslin or nylon bag. Discard the pulp. Add the sugar and chopped raisins to the liquid, and stir until the sugar is dissolved. Pour into a fermentation vessel. When lukewarm, add the wheat, sprinkle in the yeast, nutrient and additives, then follow the general instructions for fermentation and storage.

**Aerobic fermentation period
(without fermentation trap):** 3 days

**Anaerobic fermentation period
(with fermentation trap):** 4–6 weeks

Colour: Red

Classification: Dessert

Minimum storage period: 1 year

Fermentation and storage:
During the aerobic fermentation period, stir the fermenting material at least once daily, and keep it at 70°F (21°C). When the period indicated has elapsed, strain off the juice and put it into a clean vessel fitted with a fermentation trap.
During the anaerobic fermentation period, maintain the temperature above 60°F (15·5°C). When bubbling ceases and the froth dies away, rack the wine into a clean, sealed vessel.

Grape Wine

Main ingredients	4 lb. grapes, red or white 6–10 vine leaves
Other ingredients	yeast, yeast extract
Water	1 gallon (1⅕ gallon) water
Sugar	3½ lb. white sugar

Additives	citric acid, grape tannin, pectin destroying enzyme

Pour the boiling water over the grapes and vine leaves and leave for one month, mashing the grapes and stirring every day. Strain into a fermentation bowl, pressing out as much juice as possible from the grapes. Throw away the pulp. Add the sugar to the liquid and dissolve it, then the yeast, nutrient and additives. Then follow the general instructions for fermentation and storage.

**Aerobic fermentation period
(without fermentation trap):** 3 days

**Anaerobic fermentation period
(with fermentation trap):** 6 weeks

Colour: White or red

Classification: Table

Minimum storage period: 6 months

Fermentation and storage:
During the aerobic fermentation period, stir the fermenting material at least once daily, and keep it at 70°F (21°C). When the period indicated has elapsed, strain off the juice and put it into a clean vessel fitted with a fermentation trap.
During the anaerobic fermentation period, maintain the temperature above 60°F (15·5°C). When bubbling ceases and the froth dies away, rack the wine into a clean, sealed vessel.

Greengage Wine

Plum wine can be made by the same method.

Main ingredients	3 lb. greengages 6 oz. (1 cup) ground barley
Other ingredients	yeast, yeast nutrient
Water	1 gallon (1⅕ gallon) water
Sugar	3 lb. white sugar
Additives	citric acid, grape tannin, pectin destroying enzyme

Cut up the greengages, rejecting the stones, but avoid washing the fruit as this removes the natural 'bloom' which is a great help in fermentation. Put the fruit in a large bowl and add the ground barley. Pour very hot water over the fruit and barley, and leave for four days, stirring daily. Strain this mixture through your nylon bag on to the sugar; add the yeast, nutrient and additives, then follow the general instructions for fermentation and storage.
(recipe continued overleaf)

A selection of fruits from which to make wine

**Aerobic fermentation period
(without fermentation trap):** 7 days

**Anaerobic fermentation period
(with fermentation trap):** 4–6 weeks

Colour: White

Classification: Table

Minimum storage period: 6 months or longer

Fermentation and storage:
During the aerobic fermentation period, stir the fermenting material at least once daily, and keep it at 70°F (21°C). When the period indicated has elapsed, strain off the juice and put it into a clean vessel fitted with a fermentation trap.
During the anaerobic fermentation period, maintain the temperature above 60°F (15·5°C). When bubbling ceases and the froth dies away, rack the wine into a clean, sealed vessel.

Orange Wine
This recipe can also be made with six Seville oranges and six sweet oranges.

Main ingredients	**12 large sweet oranges**
	2 lemons
	1 lb. white raisins
Other ingredients	**yeast, yeast nutrient**
Water	**1 gallon (1⅕ gallon) water**
Sugar	**4 lb. white sugar**
Additives	**grape, tannin, pectin destroying enzyme**

Peel the oranges and lemons very thinly. Put half the rinds in a cool oven to dry out. Put into a bowl the orange and lemon juice, raisins and sugar, then pour over half the water and stir well. When the rinds are quite crisp, put them in a jug and pour over them the remaining boiling water. Leave to infuse for an hour, then strain off the water on to the other ingredients in the bowl. Add the yeast, nutrient and additives, then follow the general instructions for fermentation and storage.

**Aerobic fermentation period
(without fermentation trap):** 3 days

**Anaerobic fermentation period
(with fermentation trap):** 3–4 weeks

Colour: Amber

Classification: Dessert

Minimum storage period: 6 months

Fermentation and storage:
During the aerobic fermentation period, stir the fermenting material at least once daily, and keep it at 70°F (21°C). When the period indicated has elapsed,

strain off the juice and put it into a clean vessel fitted with a fermentation trap.

During the anaerobic fermentation period, maintain the temperature above 60°F (15·5°C). When bubbling ceases and the froth dies away, rack the wine into a clean, sealed vessel.

Peach Wine

Other canned fruit can be used instead of peaches, such as apricots, blackberries, blackcurrants, grapefruit, loganberries, etc.

Main ingredient	**1 lb. can of peach slices or halves, or peach pulp**
Other ingredients	**yeast, yeast nutrient**
Water	**1 gallon (1⅕ gallon) water**
Sugar	**2½ lb. white sugar**
Additives	**citric acid, grape tannin, pectin destroying enzyme**

Dissolve the sugar in some hot water, cut up the peaches into small pieces and combine with the sugar syrup; mix in the additives. Stir well, cover and leave in a warm place for 24 hours. After this period stir again, add the yeast, the nutrient and warm water to make 1 gallon. Then follow the general instructions for fermentation and storage.

Aerobic fermentation period
(without fermentation trap): 10 days

Anaerobic fermentation period
(with fermentation trap): 4 weeks

Colour: White

Classification: Table

Minimum storage period: 2 months

Fermentation and storage:
During the aerobic fermentation period, stir the fermenting material at least once daily, and keep it at 70°F (21°C). When the period indicated has elapsed, strain off the juice and put it into a clean vessel fitted with a fermentation trap.

During the anaerobic fermentation period, maintain the temperature above 60°F (15·5°C). When bubbling ceases and the froth dies away, rack the wine into a clean, sealed vessel.

Washing the pears (above left)

Cutting and weighing the pears (centre left)

Soaking the pears (left)

Pear Wine

Main ingredients	**4 lb. pears, washed**
	6 oz. (1½ cups) chopped sultanas
Other ingredients	**yeast, yeast nutrient**
Water	**1 gallon (1⅕ gallon) water**
Sugar	**3 lb. white sugar**
Additives	**citric acid, pectin destroying enzyme**
	2 Campden tablets

Cut the washed pears into pieces and put them in the cold water with the citric acid, crushed Campden tablets and pectin destroying enzyme. Cover and leave to soak for 24 hours. Add the chopped sultanas, sugar, yeast, nutrient and additives, then follow the general instructions for fermentation and storage.

Aerobic fermentation period
(without fermentation trap): 4 days

Anaerobic fermentation period
(with fermentation trap): 4–6 weeks

Colour: White

Classification: Table

Minimum storage period: 3 months

Fermentation and storage:
During the aerobic fermentation period, stir the fermenting material at least once daily, and keep it at 70°F (21°C). When the period indicated has elapsed, strain off the juice and put it into a clean vessel fitted with a fermentation trap.

During the anaerobic fermentation period, maintain the temperature above 60°F (15·5°C). When bubbling ceases and the froth dies away, rack the wine into a clean, sealed vessel.

Plum Wine

Main ingredient	**6 lb. small red or black plums**
Other ingredients	**yeast, yeast nutrient**
Water	**1 gallon (1⅕ gallon) water**
Sugar	**3 lb. white sugar**
Additives	**citric acid, grape tannin, pectin destroying enzyme**
	1 Campden tablet

Wash, stone and crush the fruit. Add boiling water, cover, and when cool add the crushed Campden tablet, sugar, yeast, nutrient and additives. Then follow the general instructions for fermentation and storage.

Aerobic fermentation period
(without fermentation trap): 3 days

Anaerobic fermentation period
(with fermentation trap): 4–6 weeks

Colour: Rosé

Classification: Table

Minimum storage period: 6 months

Fermentation and storage:
During the aerobic fermentation period, stir the fermenting material at least once daily, and keep it at 70°F (21°C). When the period indicated has elapsed, strain off the juice and put it into a clean vessel fitted with a fermentation trap.

During the anaerobic fermentation period, maintain the temperature above 60°F (15·5°C). When bubbling ceases and the froth dies away, rack the wine into a clean, sealed vessel.

Prune and Cherry Wine

Main ingredients	**2 lb. prunes**
	2 lb. ripe red or black cherries
Other ingredients	**yeast, yeast nutrient**
Water	**1 gallon (1⅕ gallon) water**
Sugar	**4 lb. demerara sugar**
Additives	**citric acid, grape tannin, pectin destroying enzyme**

Soak the prunes overnight in the water. Simmer in the same water until tender, adding the cherries for the last few minutes. Pour all into a large bowl, cover well and stir every day for ten days, pressing the fruit well against the sides of the bowl. Then strain off the liquid into another vessel, add the sugar and stir until dissolved.

Add the yeast, nutrient and additives, then follow the general instructions for fermentation and storage.

Aerobic fermentation period (without fermentation trap): 2–3 weeks

Anaerobic fermentation period (with fermentation trap): 8 weeks

Colour: Red

Classification: Table

Minimum storage period: 6 months

Fermentation and storage:
During the aerobic fermentation period, stir the fermenting material at least once daily, and keep it at 70°F (21°C). When the period indicated has elapsed, strain off the juice and put it into a clean vessel fitted with a fermentation trap.

During the anaerobic fermentation period, maintain the temperature above 60°F (15·5°C). When bubbling ceases and the froth dies away, rack the wine into a clean, sealed vessel.

Quince Wine

Main ingredient	20–25 quinces
Other ingredients	yeast, yeast nutrient 2 lemons
Water	1 gallon (1⅕ gallon) water
Sugar	3 lb. white sugar
Additives	pectin destroying enzyme

Grate the quinces into a pan, discarding the core, add the water and boil for not more than 15 minutes. Dissolve the sugar in hot water and add to the pulp with the grated skin and juice of the lemons. Cool to 70°F (21°C) and add the yeast, nutrient and additives. Then follow the general instructions for fermentation and storage.

(recipe continued overleaf)

**Aerobic fermentation period
(without fermentation trap):** 2 days

**Anaerobic fermentation period
(with fermentation trap):** 6–8 weeks

Colour: Amber

Classification: Dessert

Minimum storage period: 6 months

Fermentation and storage:
During the aerobic fermentation period, stir the fermenting material at least once daily, and keep it at 70°F (21°C). When the period indicated has elapsed, strain off the juice and put it into a clean vessel fitted with a fermentation trap.
During the anaerobic fermentation period, maintain the temperature above 60°F (15·5°C). When bubbling ceases and the froth dies away, rack the wine into a clean, sealed vessel.

Raspberry Wine

Main ingredient	**4 lb. raspberries**
Other ingredients	**yeast, yeast nutrient**
Water	**1 gallon (1⅕ gallon) water**
Sugar	**3½ lb. white sugar**
Additives	**citric acid, pectin destroying enzyme**

Put the fruit in a bowl and pour boiling water over it. When cool, break up the fruit thoroughly, cover it and leave for 3 or 4 days, stirring well once daily. Then strain on to the syrup formed by dissolving the sugar in a little hot water. Add the yeast, nutrient and additives, then follow the general instructions for fermentation and storage.

**Aerobic fermentation period
(without fermentation trap):** 2 days

**Anaerobic fermentation period
(with fermentation trap):** 6 weeks

Colour: Rosé

Classification: Table

Minimum storage period: 3–4 months

Fermentation and storage:
During the aerobic fermentation period, stir the fermenting material at least once daily, and keep it at 70°F (21°C). When the period indicated has elapsed, strain off the juice and put it into a clean vessel fitted with a fermentation trap.
During the anaerobic fermentation period, maintain the temperature above 60°F (15·5°C). When bubbling ceases and the froth dies away, rack the wine into a clean, sealed vessel.

Wine making at Pola in Istria

Colour: Rosé

Classification: Aperitif

Minimum storage period: 6 months

Fermentation and storage:
During the aerobic fermentation period, stir the fermenting material at least once daily, and keep it at 70°F (21°C). When the period indicated has elapsed, strain off the juice and put it into a clean vessel fitted with a fermentation trap.

During the anaerobic fermentation period, maintain the temperature above 60°F (15·5°C). When bubbling ceases and the froth dies away, rack the wine into a clean, sealed vessel.

Rhubarb Wine

Main ingredient	**6 lb. rhubarb (red, not the pink, forced variety)** **DO NOT USE ANY PART OF THE LEAF, WHICH IS POISONOUS**
Other ingredients	**yeast, yeast nutrient, 2 lemons**
Water	**1 gallon (1⅕ gallon) water**
Sugar	**3½ lb. white sugar**
Additives	**grape tannin, pectin destroying enzyme, 1 Campden tablet, 1 oz. precipitated chalk**

Cut up and crush the rhubarb. Cover with cold water and add the crushed Campden tablet. Leave for 3 days, stirring frequently, then strain and add the precipitated chalk to the juice—which will fizz. This removes excess oxalic acid. Then add the sugar, yeast, nutrient, lemon juice and other additives and follow the general instructions for fermentation and storage.

**Aerobic fermentation period
(without fermentation trap):** 3 days

**Anaerobic fermentation period
(with fermentation trap):** 4–6 weeks

Colour: Rosé

Classification: Table

Minimum storage period: 6 months

Fermentation and storage:
During the aerobic fermentation period, stir the fermenting material at least once daily, and keep it at 70°F (21°C). When the period indicated has elapsed, strain off the juice and put it into a clean vessel fitted with a fermentation trap.

During the anaerobic fermentation period, maintain the temperature above 60°F (15·5°C). When bubbling ceases and the froth dies away, rack the wine into a clean, sealed vessel.

Redcurrant Wine

Main ingredient	**2 lb. redcurrants**
Other ingredients	**yeast, yeast nutrient**
Water	**1 gallon (1⅕ gallon) water**
Sugar	**3½ lb. white sugar**
Additives	**citric acid, grape tannin, pectin destroying enzyme**

Pour the boiling water over the redcurrants and let them stand for four or five days, squeezing and stirring every day. Then strain carefully, taking care to get all the juice from the pulp before throwing it away. Add the sugar to this liquid and stir until dissolved. Add the yeast, nutrient and additives, then follow the general instructions for fermentation and storage.

**Aerobic fermentation period
(without fermentation trap):** 14 days

**Anaerobic fermentation period
(with fermentation trap):** 4 weeks

Rhubarb and Beetroot Wine

Main ingredients	**3 lb. rhubarb**
	3 lb. beetroot
	1 lb. wheat
Other ingredients	**yeast, yeast nutrient**
	1 oz. root ginger
Water	**1 gallon (1½ gallon) water**
Sugar	**4 lb. white sugar**
Additives	**grape tannin, pectin destroying enzyme**

Cut the rhubarb into small pieces but do not peel it. Put it in a bowl and pour half a gallon (4⅘ pint) of boiling water over it. Let it stand for 10 days, stirring and pressing the fruit every day, then strain well and press all the liquid from the rhubarb.

Wash the beetroot and boil it in half a gallon of water; when tender, strain out the liquid into the rhubarb liquid. Put all into the fermentation vessel and add the root ginger (well bruised), the sugar and raisins; stir the mixture well until the sugar dissolves. Add the wheat, yeast, nutrient and additives, then follow the general instructions for fermentation and storage.

Aerobic fermentation period (without fermentation trap): 3 weeks

Anaerobic fermentation period (with fermentation trap): 4–6 weeks

Colour: Rosé

Classification: Table

Minimum storage period: 6 months

Fermentation and storage:
During the aerobic fermentation period, stir the fermenting material at least once daily, and keep it at 70°F (21°C). When the period indicated has elapsed, strain off the juice and put it into a clean vessel fitted with a fermentation trap.

During the anaerobic fermentation period, maintain the temperature above 60°F (15·5°C). When bubbling ceases and the froth dies away, rack the wine into a clean, sealed vessel.

Strawberry Wine

Main ingredient	**4 lb. strawberries**
Other ingredients	**yeast, yeast nutrient**
Water:	**1 gallon (1⅕ gallon) water**
Sugar	**3 lb. white sugar**
Additives	**citric acid, grape tannin**

Core and wash the strawberries well, then mash them with the sugar dissolved in a little hot water. Add half the water and leave for two days. Strain the liquor off into the fermenting jar, add the rest of the water to the pulp, mix well and strain off again into the fermenting jar. Add the yeast, nutrient and additives, then follow the general instructions for fermentation and storage.

**Aerobic fermentation period
(without fermentation trap):** 1 day

**Anaerobic fermentation period
(with fermentation trap):** 4–5 weeks

Colour: Rosé

Classification: Table

Minimum storage period: 3 months

Fermentation and storage:
During the aerobic fermentation period, stir the fermenting material at least once daily, and keep it at 70°F (21°C). When the period indicated has elapsed, strain off the juice and put it into a clean vessel fitted with a fermentation trap.

During the anaerobic fermentation period, maintain the temperature above 60°F (15·5°C). When bubbling ceases and the froth dies away, rack the wine into a clean, sealed vessel.

Dried Apricot Wine

The advantage of this wine is that it can be made all the year round. Any apricots left over after soaking can be used in desserts. A good apricot brandy can be made by adding 5–6 (10–12) tablespoons of commercial brandy to your bottle of apricot wine. A little sugar syrup may be necessary to bring the liqueur to the correct sweetness, but this is largely a matter of taste.

Main ingredients	**1 lb. dried apricots**
	1 lb. chopped raisins
Other ingredients	**yeast, yeast nutrient**
	$\frac{1}{4}$ pint ($\frac{5}{8}$ cup) strong tea
	juice and rind of one lemon
Water	**1 gallon (1$\frac{1}{2}$ gallon) water**
Sugar	**3 lb. demerara sugar**
Additives	**citric acid, pectin destroying enzyme**

Wash the apricots, cut them into quarters and soak them overnight in one pint (2$\frac{1}{2}$ cups) of the water. Put the apricot quarters and chopped raisins into a fermenting bowl. Boil half the sugar in four pints of water and pour over the fruit. Add the strained tea and leave the mixture to cool. Put the juice and rind of the lemon into the fermenting bowl. Add the rest of the water, yeast, nutrient and additives, then follow the general instructions for fermentation and storage.

**Aerobic fermentation period
(without fermentation trap):** 8 days

**Anaerobic fermentation period
(with fermentation trap):** 6 weeks

Colour: Golden

Classification: Dessert

Minimum storage period: 6–8 months

Fermentation and storage:
During the aerobic fermentation period, stir the fermenting material at least once daily, and keep it at 70°F (21°C). When the period indicated has elapsed, strain off the juice and put it into a clean vessel fitted with a fermentation trap.
During the anaerobic fermentation period, maintain the temperature above 60°F (15·5°C). When bubbling ceases and the froth dies away, rack the wine into a clean, sealed vessel.

Dried Bilberry Wine

Main ingredients	**1 lb. dried bilberries**
	1 lb. chopped raisins
Other ingredients	**yeast, yeast nutrient**
	rind and juice of 3 lemons
Water	**1 gallon (1$\frac{1}{5}$ gallon) water**
Sugar	**3 lb. white sugar**
Additives	**pectin destroying enzyme**
	$\frac{1}{2}$ Campden tablet

Wash the bilberries under running cold water. Then soak the bilberries in 2 pints of water in a bowl, keeping the bowl covered. Boil half the sugar in three pint (3$\frac{3}{5}$ pint) of water for one minute. Cool, then mix with the bilberries and any water that may be left with them. Add the chopped raisins and water to 1 gallon (1$\frac{1}{5}$ gallon) of water. Add both peel and juice of the lemons to the bilberries with the yeast, yeast nutrient, sugar and additives, then follow the general instructions for fermentation and storage.

**Aerobic fermentation period
(without fermentation trap):** 7 days

**Anaerobic fermentation period
(with fermentation trap):** 6–8 weeks

Colour: Red

Classification: Dessert

Minimum storage period: 6 months

Fermentation and storage:
During the aerobic fermentation period, stir the fermenting material at least once daily, and keep it at 70°F (21°C). When the period indicated has elapsed, strain off the juice and put it into a clean vessel fitted with a fermentation trap.
During the anaerobic fermentation period, maintain the temperature above 60°F (15·5°C). When bubbling ceases and the froth dies away, rack the wine into a clean, sealed vessel.

Date Wine

Main ingredient	**1 lb. dates**
Other ingredients	**yeast, yeast nutrient**
	$\frac{1}{2}$ lb. barley
	1 orange
	1 lemon
Water	**1 gallon (1$\frac{1}{5}$ gallon) water**
Sugar	**3 lb. white sugar**
Additives	**citric acid, $\frac{1}{2}$ nutmeg**

Peel the orange and lemon thinly, avoiding the pith which would make the wine bitter. Chop the dates. Boil the water, add the orange, lemon, dates and barley and continue boiling for 10 minutes, then add half a nutmeg, not grated. Boil for another 15 minutes then strain on to the sugar, stirring well. Cool to 70°F (21°C), add the yeast, nutrient and additives, then follow the general instructions for fermentation and storage.

**Aerobic fermentation period
(without fermentation trap):** 5 days

**Anaerobic fermentation period
(with fermentation trap):** 4 weeks

Colour: Amber

Classification: Dessert

Minimum storage period: 3–4 months

Fermentation and storage:
During the aerobic fermentation period, stir the fermenting material at least once daily, and keep it at 70°F (21°C). When the period indicated has elapsed, strain off the juice and put it into a clean vessel fitted with a fermentation trap.
During the anaerobic fermentation period, maintain the temperature above 60°F (15·5°C). When bubbling ceases and the froth dies away, rack the wine into a clean, sealed vessel.

Fig Wine

Main ingredients	2 lb. dried figs ½ lb. chopped raisins
Other ingredients	yeast, yeast nutrient rind and juice of 1 large lemon rind and juice of 1 orange
Water	1 gallon (1⅕ gallon) water
Sugar	2½ lb. brown sugar
Additives	citric acid, grape tannin, pectin destroying enzyme

Chop up the figs and raisins, add the rinds of the lemon and orange and the boiling water. Stand for two days then stir in the brown sugar and, when cool, add the yeast, nutrient, additives, lemon and orange juice, then follow the general instructions for fermentation and storage.

**Aerobic fermentation period
(without fermentation trap):** 1 week

**Anaerobic fermentation period
(with fermentation trap):** 6–8 weeks

Colour: Amber

Classification: Dessert

Minimum storage period: 6 months or longer

Fermentation and storage:
During the aerobic fermentation period, stir the fer-

62

menting material at least once daily, and keep it at 70°F (21°C). When the period indicated has elapsed, strain off the juice and put it into a clean vessel fitted with a fermentation trap.
During the anaerobic fermentation period, maintain the temperature above 60°F (15·5°C). When bubbling ceases and the froth dies away, rack the wine into a clean, sealed vessel.

Mixed Dried Fruit Wine

Main ingredients	4 oz. (1 cup) currants 4 oz. (1 cup) white raisins 2 oz. (½ cup) chopped sultanas 2 oz. (½ cup) finely chopped candied peel 1 lb. wheat grains
Other ingredients	yeast, yeast nutrient
Water	1 gallon (1⅕ gallon) water
Sugar	3 lb. white sugar
Additives	citric acid, grape tannin, pectin destroying enzyme

Mix the fruit and candied peel, but do not wash it. Put it in a large basin with the sugar and the wheat, and pour the boiling water over it, stirring well to dissolve the sugar. When lukewarm, add the yeast, nutrient and additives, then follow the general instructions for fermentation and storage.

**Aerobic fermentation period
(without fermentation trap):** 3 weeks

**Anaerobic fermentation period
(with fermentation trap):** 3 weeks

Colour: Amber

Classification: Dessert

Minimum storage period: 6 months

Fermentation and storage:
During the aerobic fermentation period, stir the fermenting material at least once daily, and keep it at 70°F (21°C). When the period indicated has elapsed, strain off the juice and put it into a clean vessel fitted with a fermentation trap.
During the anaerobic fermentation period, maintain the temperature above 60°F (15·5°C). When bubbling ceases and the froth dies away, rack the wine into a clean, sealed vessel.

Some ingredients for dried fruit wines

Fruit Wines using Concentrates

The recipe below is typical. If instructions on the label differ, follow those on the label.

Main ingredient	**1 gallon fruit juice—apple, pear, etc., as available**
Other ingredients	**yeast, yeast nutrient**
Water	**3 gallon (3⅗ gallon) water**
Sugar	**5 lb. white sugar**
Additives	**citric acid, grape tannin, pectin destroying enzyme**

Dissolve the sugar in hot water, and add to the concentrate in a fermenting jar. Add the yeast, nutrient and additives, then follow the general instructions for fermentation and storage. For this wine there is no aerobic fermentation period.

**Anaerobic fermentation period
(with fermentation trap):** 4–5 weeks

Colour: White

Classification: Table or dessert

Minimum storage period: 5–6 weeks

Fermentation and storage:
During the anaerobic fermentation period, maintain the temperature above 60°F (15·5°C). When bubbling ceases and the froth dies away, rack the wine into a clean, sealed vessel.

Vin Ordinaire

All concentrated grape juices are fermented in a similar way, but follow the instructions given on the container.

Main ingredient	**1 can red or white grape juice concentrate**
Other ingredient	**yeast**
Water	**1 gallon (1⅕ gallon) water**
Sugar	**10 oz. white sugar**

Pour the can of juice concentrate into a gallon container, and add 5 oz. of sugar previously dissolved in hot water. Rinse out all the sediment from the can and add to the container, then fill up to nearly 1 gallon with lukewarm water. Add the yeast and fix a fermentation trap. For this wine there is no aerobic fermentation period. After ten days add the remaining 5 oz. of sugar, then follow the general instructions for fermentation and storage.

**Anaerobic fermentation period
(with fermentation trap):** 4–5 weeks

Colour: Red, white or rosé

64

Classification: Table

Minimum storage period: 4 weeks

Fermentation and storage:
During the anaerobic fermentation period, maintain the temperature above 60°F (15·5°C). When bubbling ceases and the froth dies away, rack the wine into a clean, sealed vessel.

Beetroot Wine

In making beetroot wine it is important that light should be excluded, otherwise the wine will turn brown instead of the bright red it should be.

Main ingredient	**4 lb. beetroot**
Other ingredients	**yeast, yeast nutrient, juice of 1 lemon, 4 cloves 1 oz. bruised root ginger**
Water	**1 gallon (1½ gallon) water**
Sugar	**3½ lb. white sugar**
Additives	**citric acid, grape tannin**

Wash the beetroot, but do not peel. Slice quickly into the water and cook gently until tender but not mushy. Strain on to the sugar, lemon juice, cloves and bruised ginger. Add the yeast, nutrient and additives, then follow the general instructions for fermentation and storage.

**Aerobic fermentation period
(without fermentation trap):** 3 days

**Anaerobic fermentation period
(with fermentation trap):** 3–4 months

Colour: Red

Classification: Table

Minimum storage period: 3 months

Fermentation and storage:
During the aerobic fermentation period, stir the fermenting material at least once daily, and keep it at 70°F (21°C). When the period indicated has elapsed, strain off the juice and put it into a clean vessel fitted with a fermentation trap.
During the anaerobic fermentation period, maintain the temperature above 60°F (15·5°C). When bubbling ceases and the froth dies away, rack the wine into a clean, sealed vessel.

Rhubarb wine

Broad Bean Wine

Main ingredients	4 lb. shelled old broad beans
	4 oz. chopped sultanas
Other ingredients	yeast, yeast nutrient
	rind and juice of 1 lemon
Water	1 gallon (1⅕ gallon) water
Sugar	2¾ lb. white sugar
Additives	citric acid, grape tannin

Boil the beans gently in the gallon of water, with the lemon rind, for one hour. Strain, add the chopped sultanas to the liquid and stir in the sugar. When cool add the lemon juice, yeast, nutrient and additives. Then follow the general instructions for fermentation and storage.

Aerobic fermentation period (without fermentation trap): 2 weeks, then strain off sultanas

Anaerobic fermentation period (with fermentation trap): 4–6 weeks

Colour: White

Classification: Table

Minimum storage period: 6 months

Fermentation and storage:
During the aerobic fermentation period, stir the fermenting material at least once daily, and keep it at 70°F (21°C). When the period indicated has elapsed, strain off the juice and put it into a clean vessel fitted with a fermentation trap.

During the anaerobic fermentation period, maintain the temperature above 60°F (15·5°C). When bubbling ceases and the froth dies away, rack the wine into a clean, sealed vessel.

Carrot Wine

Half an ounce of dried hops can be added to the boiling to give some more 'bite' to this wine, if desired.

Main ingredients	**6 lb. carrots**
	4 oranges
	4 lemons
	½ lb. chopped raisins
Other ingredients	**yeast, yeast nutrient**
Water	**1 gallon (1⅕ gallon) water**
Sugar	**4 lb. demerara sugar**
Additives	**½ teaspoon black pepper, grape tannin**

The carrots should be large but not woody. Do not peel, but wash them well and cut off the dark circles at the larger end where the leaves have grown. Grate them and put them with the water in a large pan. Bring to a rapid boil and continue boiling steadily for 40 minutes. Leave to cool and when lukewarm, strain through your nylon bag into a fermentation bowl, squeezing well to remove as much liquid as possible.

Add the sugar and stir until it all dissolves, then add the sliced oranges and lemons, chopped raisins and black pepper. Add the yeast, nutrient and other additives, then follow the general instructions for fermentation and storage.

Aerobic fermentation period (without fermentation trap): 2 weeks

Anaerobic fermentation period (with fermentation trap): 4–6 weeks

Colour: Rosé

Classification: Table

Minimum storage period: 6–9 months

Fermentation and storage:
During the aerobic fermentation period, stir the fermenting material at least once daily, and keep it at 70°F (21°C). When the period indicated has elapsed, strain off the juice and put it into a clean vessel fitted with a fermentation trap.

During the anaerobic fermentation period, maintain the temperature above 60°F (15·5°C). When bubbling ceases and the froth dies away, rack the wine into a clean, sealed vessel.

illustrations on pages 68 and 69:

Carrot wine (left)

Celery wine (right)

Celery Wine

Main ingredients	**4 lb. celery (use both green and white parts of the stems, but not the leaves)** **½ lb. chopped sultanas**
Other ingredients	**yeast, yeast nutrient** **juice of 2 large lemons**
Water	**1 gallon (1⅓ gallon) water**
Sugar	**3 lb. brown sugar**
Additives	**citric acid, grape tannin**

Wash the celery, cut it into short lengths and boil it in the water until just tender, then strain the water onto the sultanas in a fermentation bowl. Make up the quantity to one gallon with hot water. Add the sugar and lemon juice, and stir until dissolved. When the water is lukewarm, stir in the yeast, nutrient and additives, then follow the general instructions for fermentation and storage.

**Aerobic fermentation period
(without fermentation trap):** 12 days

**Anaerobic fermentation period
(with fermentation trap):** 3 weeks

Colour: White

Classification: Table

Minimum storage period: 6 months

Fermentation and storage:
During the aerobic fermentation period, stir the fermenting material at least once daily, and keep it at 70°F (21°C). When the period indicated has elapsed, strain off the juice and put it into a clean vessel fitted with a fermentation trap.
During the anaerobic fermentation period, maintain the temperature above 60°F (15·5°C). When bubbling ceases and the froth dies away, rack the wine into a clean, sealed vessel.

Parsley Wine

Main ingredients	**1 lb. fresh parsley** **2 lemons** **2 oranges**
Other ingredients	**yeast, yeast nutrient** **½ oz. green ginger** **¼ pint (⅝ cup) cold tea**
Water	**1 gallon (1⅓ gallon) water**
Sugar	**3 lb. white sugar**
Additives	**citric acid, grape tannin, pectin destroying enzyme**

Boil in the water the parsley, ginger (well bruised), and
70

the rinds and juice of the lemons and oranges, for 15 minutes. Strain on to the sugar and stir until the sugar has dissolved. When lukewarm, add the cold tea, yeast, nutrient and then follow the general instructions for fermentation and storage.

**Aerobic fermentation period
(without fermentation trap):** 2 days

**Anaerobic fermentation period
(with fermentation trap):** 4–6 weeks

Colour: White

Classification: Table

Minimum storage period: 6 months

Fermentation and storage:
During the aerobic fermentation period, stir the fermenting material at least once daily, and keep it at 70°F (21°C). When the period indicated has elapsed, strain off the juice and put it into a clean vessel fitted with a fermentation trap.
During the anaerobic fermentation period, maintain the temperature above 60°F (15·5°C). When bubbling ceases and the froth dies away, rack the wine into a clean, sealed vessel.

Parsnip Wine

Main ingredient	**5 lb. parsnips**
Other ingredients	**yeast, yeast nutrient** **⅓ pint (⅝ cup) cold tea** **1 oz. bruised root ginger** **rind and juice of 1 lemon**
Water	**1 gallon (1⅓ gallon) water**
Sugar	**3 lb. white sugar**
Additives	**citric acid, pectin destroying enzyme** **1 Campden tablet**

Wash and peel the parsnips, cut them up roughly and boil them in the water until tender but not mushy. Strain through a sieve into another bowl, but do not press the parsnips or the wine will be cloudy and impossible to clear. Add the sugar and ginger, and boil until the sugar has dissolved. Add the lemon juice and thinly-pared rind, the cold tea and crushed Campden tablet. When lukewarm add the yeast nutrient and additives. Then follow the general instructions for fermentation and storage.

**Aerobic fermentation period
(without fermentation trap):** 2 weeks

**Anaerobic fermentation period
(with fermentation trap):** 6 months

A selection of country vegetables from which to make wine

Colour: White

Classification: Table

Minimum storage period: 3 months

Fermentation and storage:
During the aerobic fermentation period, stir the fermenting material at least once daily, and keep it at 70°F (21°C). When the period indicated has elapsed, strain off the juice and put it into a clean vessel fitted with a fermentation trap.

During the anaerobic fermentation period, maintain the temperature above 60°F (15·5°C). When bubbling ceases and the froth dies away, rack the wine into a clean, sealed vessel.

Pea Pod Wine

Main ingredient	**4–5 lb. pea pods**
Other ingredients	**yeast, yeast nutrient**
Water	**1 gallon (1⅕ gallon) water**
Sugar	**3 lb. white sugar**
Additives	**citric acid, grape tannin, pectin destroying enzyme** **1 Campden tablet**

The pea pods should by young and fleshy; withered pods are no good. Wash them well in water to which one crushed Campden tablet has been added. Boil them in the water until they are tender, then strain, and dissolve the sugar in the hot liquid. Add the yeast, nutrient and additives, then follow the general instructions for fermentation and storage.

Aerobic fermentation period
(without fermentation trap): 3 days

Anaerobic fermentation period
(with fermentation trap): 4–6 weeks

Colour: White

Classification: Table

Minimum storage period: 6 months

Fermentation and storage:
During the aerobic fermentation period, stir the fermenting material at least once daily, and keep it at 70°F (21°C). When the period indicated has elapsed, strain off the juice and put it into a clean vessel fitted with a fermentation trap.

During the anaerobic fermentation period, maintain the temperature above 60°F (15·5°C). When bubbling ceases and the froth dies away, rack the wine into a clean, sealed vessel.

Turnip wine (right)
72

Potato Wine

Main ingredients	**4 lb. potatoes** **juice and rind of 1 orange** **juice and rind of 1 lemon** **½ lb. wheat** **½ lb. raisins**
Other ingredients	**yeast, yeast nutrient**
Water	**1 gallon (1⅕ gallon) water**
Sugar	**3 lb. white sugar**
Additives	**citric acid, grape tannin, pectin destroying enzyme**

Wash and peel the potatoes and cook gently in the water until soft. Strain the water on to the rind and juice of the orange and lemon, and add to this the wheat, sugar and raisins. When the liquid has cooled a little, add the yeast, nutrient and additives, then follow the general instructions for fermentation and storage.

Aerobic fermentation period
(without fermentation trap): 3 weeks

Anaerobic fermentation period
(with fermentation trap): 4–6 weeks

Colour: White

Classification: Table

Minimum storage period: 6–8 months

Fermentation and storage:
During the aerobic fermentation period, stir the fermenting material at least once daily, and keep it at 70°F (21°C). When the period indicated has elapsed, strain off the juice and put it into a clean vessel fitted with a fermentation trap.

During the anaerobic fermentation period, maintain the temperature above 60°F (15·5°C). When bubbling ceases and the froth dies away, rack the wine into a clean, sealed vessel.

Turnip Wine

Main ingredient	**1 gallon (1⅕ gallon) chopped mangolds or swedes (rutalsaga)**
Other ingredients	**yeast, yeast nutrient** **½ oz. dried hops**
Water	**1 gallon (1⅕ gallon) water**
Sugar	**3 lb. white sugar**
Additives	**citric acid, grape tannin, pectin destroying enzyme**

Wash the vegetables well, removing any tough tops or rough roots. Cut them up roughly and boil in the water for one hour, then strain. Add the sugar to the hot

liquid and stir until dissolved. Now add the hops, and, when the mixture is lukewarm, the yeast, nutrient and additives. Then follow the general instructions for fermentation and storage.

Aerobic fermentation period
(without fermentation trap): 3–4 days

Anaeroblic fermentation period
(with fermentation trap): 4–6 weeks

Colour: White

Classification: Table

Minimum storage period: 6 months

Fermentation and storage:
During the aerobic fermentation period, stir the fermenting material at least once daily, and keep it at 70°F (21°C). When the period indicated has elapsed, strain off the juice and put it into a clean vessel fitted with a fermentation trap.
During the anaerobic fermentation period, maintain the temperature above 60°F (15·5°C). When bubbling ceases and the froth dies away, rack the wine into a clean, sealed vessel.

Almond Wine

Main ingredients	**2 oz. (¼ cup) skinned almonds** **1 lb. dark raisins**
Other ingredients	**yeast, yeast nutrient,** **rind and juice of 3 lemons**
Water	**1 gallon (1⅕ gallon) water**
Sugar	**3 lb. brown sugar**
Additives	**grape tannin**

Chop the almonds and raisins and simmer in the water for one hour, then strain into fermentation vessel and make up to 1 gallon (1⅕ gallon) with boiling water. Add the sugar and stir until dissolved, then add the juice and rind of the lemons. When lukewarm, add the yeast, nutrient and additive, then follow the general instructions for fermentation and storage.

Aerobic fermentation period
(without fermentation trap): 14 days

Anaerobic fermentation period
(with fermentation trap): 3 weeks

Colour: Medium

Classification: Dessert

Minimum storage period: 6 months

Fermentation and storage:
During the aerobic fermentation period, stir the fermenting material at least once daily, and keep it at 70°F (21°C). When the period indicated has elapsed, strain off the juice and put it into a clean vessel fitted with a fermentation trap.
During the anaerobic fermentation period, maintain the temperature above 60°F (15·5°C). When bubbling ceases and the froth dies away, rack the wine into a clean, sealed vessel.

Clove Wine

Main ingredient	**1 oz. cloves**
Other ingredients	**yeast, yeast nutrient** **1 oz. ginger** **3 lemons** **1 orange**
Water	**1 gallon (1⅕ gallon) water**
Sugar	**3 lb. brown sugar**
Additive	**citric acid**

Grate the lemon and orange peel thinly and put it into a muslin bag with the cloves and bruised ginger. Boil up the water, drop in the bag and simmer for 1 hour. Add the sugar and stir well. Cool to 70°F (21°C), add the yeast, nutrient and acid, then follow the general instructions for fermentation and storage.

Aerobic fermentation period
(without fermentation trap): 4 days

Anaerobic fermentation period
(with fermentation trap): 4–5 weeks

Colour: Amber

Classification: Dessert

Minimum storage period: 6 months

Fermentation and storage:
During the aerobic fermentation period, stir the fermenting material at least once daily, and keep it at 70°F (21°C). When the period indicated has elapsed, strain off the juice and put it into a clean vessel fitted with a fermentation trap.
During the anaerobic fermentation period, maintain the temperature above 60°F (15·5°C). When bubbling ceases and the froth dies away, rack the wine into a clean, sealed vessel.

Ginger Wine

If you like it really hot, add ½ oz. capsicum essence to the must.

Main ingredient	**3 oz. root ginger**
Other ingredients	**yeast, yeast nutrient** **2 oranges, 2 lemons** **½ lb. raisins**
Water	**1 gallon (1⅕ gallon) water**
Sugar	**3½ lb. white sugar**
Additive	**citric acid**

Peel the oranges and lemons thinly, avoiding the pith which makes wine bitter. Combine this peel with the juice of the fruit and the chopped raisins. Boil the water, add the sugar and crushed ginger, and keep boiling for 30 minutes. Add the rinds and fruit, cool to 70°F (21°C), add the yeast, nutrient and additives; then follow the general instructions for fermentation and storage.

**Aerobic fermentation period
(without fermentation trap):** 10 days

**Anaerobic fermentation period
(with fermentation trap):** 2 weeks

Colour: Amber

Classification: Dessert

Minimum storage period: 3 months

Fermentation and storage:
During the aerobic fermentation period, stir the fermenting material at least once daily, and keep it at 70°F (21°C). When the period indicated has elapsed, strain off the juice and put it into a clean vessel fitted with a fermentation trap.
During the anaerobic fermentation period, maintain the temperature above 60°F (15·5°C). When bubbling ceases and the froth dies away, rack the wine into a clean, sealed vessel.

Coffee Wine

Main ingredient	**½ lb. roasted, ground coffee**
Other ingredients	**yeast, yeast nutrient** **2 lemons**
Water	**1 gallon (1⅕ gallon) water**
Sugar	**3 lb. white sugar**
Additive	**citric acid**

Grate the lemon peel thinly (avoiding the pith, which would make the wine bitter) and boil the peel and coffee together for 30 minutes. Add the sugar and stir well. When cooled to 70°F (21°C), add the yeast, nutrient and additive, and the juice of the lemons. Then follow the general instructions for fermentation and storage.

**Aerobic fermentation period
(without fermentation trap):** 7 days

**Anaerobic fermentation period
(with fermentation trap):** 4–5 weeks

Colour: Amber

Classification: Table or dessert

Minimum storage period: 2–3 months

Fermentation and storage:
During the aerobic fermentation period, stir the fermenting material at least once daily, and keep it at 70°F (21°C). When the period indicated has elapsed, strain off the juice and put it into a clean vessel fitted with a fermentation trap.
During the anaerobic fermentation period, maintain the temperature above 60°F (15·5°C). When bubbling ceases and the froth dies away, rack the wine into a clean, sealed vessel.

Tea Wine

Main ingredient	**4 tablespoons (5T) dry tea, Indian or China. The scented teas are recommended**
Other ingredients	**yeast, yeast nutrient**
Water	**1 gallon (1⅕ gallon) water**
Sugar	**2½ lb. white sugar**
Additive	**citric acid**

Thoroughly warm a bowl, put the tea and sugar together in it, and then pour over the water, which should be boiling quickly. Allow to infuse until cool, then strain into the fermenting vessel, adding the yeast, nutrient and additive, then follow the general instructions for fermentation and storage. For this wine there is no aerobic fermentation period.

**Anaerobic fermentation period
(with fermentation trap):** 4–5 weeks

Colour: Amber

Classification: Table

Minimum storage period: 2 months

Fermentation and storage:
During the anaerobic fermentation period, maintain the temperature above 60°F (15·5°C). When bubbling ceases and the froth dies away, rack the wine into a clean, sealed vessel.

Parsley wine

Clover Wine

Main ingredients	**4 lb. pink clover flowers** **2 lemons** **2 oranges**
Other ingredients	**yeast, yeast extract** **1 oz root ginger**
Water	**1 gallon (1⅕ gallon) water**
Sugar	**3 lb. white sugar**
Additives	**citric acid, grape tannin, pectin** **destroying enzyme**

Put the flowers, water and sugar into a pan. Add the lemon and orange rinds, with all the pith removed, and the squeezed-out juice. Add the ginger (which should be well bruised), and bring the mixture to the boil. Simmer gently for half an hour, stirring from time to time. Then strain into your fermentation vessel. When the mixture is lukewarm, add the yeast, nutrient and additives. Then follow the general instructions for fermentation and storage.

Aerobic fermentation period
(without fermentation trap): 14 days

Anaerobic fermentation period
(with fermentation trap): 4–6 weeks

Colour: White

Classification: Table

Minimum storage period: 6 months

Fermentation and storage:
During the aerobic fermentation period, stir the fermenting material at least once daily, and keep it at 70°F (21°C). When the period indicated has elapsed, strain off the juice and put it into a clean vessel fitted with a fermentation trap.
During the anaerobic fermentation period, maintain the temperature above 60°F (15·5°C). When bubbling ceases and the froth dies away, rack the wine into a clean, sealed vessel.

Cowslip Wine

Main ingredients	**1 gallon (1⅕ gallon) cowslip flowers** **2 oranges** **1 lemon**
Other ingredients	**yeast, yeast nutrient**
Water	**1 gallon (1⅕ gallon) water**
Sugar	**3 lb. white sugar**
Additives	**citric acid, grape tannin, pectin destroying enzyme**

Use only the yellow parts of the flowers. Boil the water and dissolve the sugar in it. Put in a bowl the thinly-pared orange and lemon rinds, and pour the hot syrup over them. When lukewarm, add the flowers, the juice of the oranges and lemon, and the remaining ingredients. Then follow the general instructions for fermentation and storage.

**Aerobic fermentation period
(without fermentation trap):** 4 days

**Anaerobic fermentation period
(with fermentation trap):** 3 months

Colour: White

Classification: Table

Minimum storage period: 9 months

Fermentation and storage:

During the aerobic fermentation period, stir the fermenting material at least once daily, and keep it at 70°F (21°C). When the period indicated has elapsed, strain off the juice and put it into a clean vessel fitted with a fermentation trap.

During the anaerobic fermentation period, maintain the temperature above 60°F (15·5°C). When bubbling ceases and the froth dies away, rack the wine into a clean, sealed vessel.

Dandelion Wine

Main ingredients	**3 quarts ($\frac{3}{5}$ gallon) dandelion flowers** **rind and juice of 1 lemon** **rind and juice of 1 orange**
Other ingredients	**yeast, yeast nutrient** **1 oz. root ginger**
Water	**1 gallon ($1\frac{1}{5}$ gallon) water**
Sugar	**3 lb. white sugar**
Additives	**citric acid, grape tannin, pectin destroying enzyme**

Wash the flowers, put them in a bowl and cover with boiling water; cover the bowl and leave for three days, stirring every day. Do not exceed three days. Squeeze out the flowers and put the liquid in a pan with the rind (yellow part only), the juice of the lemon and orange, the sugar and the ginger (which should be well bruised); boil for 30 minutes. Pour into the bowl and leave to cool, add the yeast, nutrient and additives, then follow the general instructions for fermentation and storage.

Aerobic fermentation period (without fermentation trap): 6 days

Anaerobic fermentation period (with fermentation trap): 3 months

Colour: White

Classification: Table

Minimum storage period: 9 months

Fermentation and storage:
During the aerobic fermentation period, stir the fermenting material at least once daily, and keep it at 70°F (21°C). When the period indicated has elapsed, strain off the juice and put it into a clean vessel with a trap. During the anaerobic fermentation period, maintain the temperature above 60°F (15·5°C). When bubbling ceases and the froth dies away, rack the wine into a clean, sealed vessel.

Elderflower Wine

Main ingredients	**2 pints (5 cups) elderflowers (stripped of all green parts)** **4 oz. white raisins** **1 orange** **1 lemon**
Other ingredients	**yeast, yeast nutrient**
Water	**1 gallon ($1\frac{1}{5}$ gallon) water**
Sugar	**2 lb. white sugar**
Additives	**citric acid, grape tannin, pectin destroying enzyme**

Add to the water the thinly pared rinds of the orange and lemon, and the raisins, and bring to the boil. When boiling, add the sugar and stir until dissolved. Simmer for 10 minutes. Put the blossoms into a large bowl and pour the hot syrup, rinds and raisins over them. Leave to cool until lukewarm; add the juice of the orange and lemon, then add the yeast, nutrient and additives. Then follow the general instructions for fermentation and storage.

Aerobic fermentation period (without fermentation trap): 6 days

Anaerobic fermentation period (with fermentation trap): 4 weeks

Colour: Red

Classification: Table

Minimum storage period: 6 months

Fermentation and storage:
During the aerobic fermentation period, stir the fermenting material at least once daily, and keep it at 70°F (21°C). When the period indicated has elapsed, strain off the juice and put it into a clean vessel fitted with a fermentation trap.
During the anaerobic fermentation period, maintain the temperature above 60°F (15·5°C). When bubbling ceases and the froth dies away, rack the wine into a clean, sealed vessel.

Hawthorn Wine

Main ingredients	**1 gallon ($1\frac{1}{5}$ gallon) May hawthorn blossom** **$\frac{1}{2}$ lb. chopped raisins** **$\frac{1}{2}$ lb. wheat**
Other ingredients	**yeast, yeast nutrient**
Water	**$1\frac{1}{2}$ gallon ($1\frac{4}{5}$ gallon) water**
Sugar	**3 lb. white sugar**
Additives	**citric acid, grape tannin, pectin destroying enzyme**

Put the blossoms in a bowl. Boil the water and sugar together and pour over the flowers. Stir well and leave to cool. When lukewarm, add the chopped raisins and the wheat, stir well and add the yeast, nutrient and additives; then follow the general instructions for fermentation and storage.

Aerobic fermentation period (without fermentation trap): 16 days

Anaerobic fermentation period (with fermentation trap): 4–6 weeks

Colour: White

Classification: Table

Minimum storage period: 6 months

Fermentation and storage:

During the aerobic fermentation period, stir the fermenting material at least once daily, and keep it at 70°F (21°C). When the period indicated has elapsed, strain off the juice and put it into a clean vessel fitted with a fermentation trap.

During the anaerobic fermentation period, maintain the temperature above 60°F (15·5°C). When bubbling ceases and the froth dies away, rack the wine into a clean, sealed vessel.

Honeysuckle Wine

Main ingredient	**2 pints blossom, fully open and dry**
Other ingredients	**yeast, yeast nutrient**
	4 oz. raisins
	1 lemon
	1 orange
Water	**1 gallon (1¼ gallon) water**
Sugar	**3 lb. white sugar**
Additives	**citric acid, grape tannin**
	1 Campden tablet

Wash the flowers, add the water, the dissolved sugar syrup, chopped raisins, the juice of the orange and lemon, and a crushed Campden tablet. Let stand for one day, then add the yeast, nutrient and additives. Then follow the general instructions for fermentation and storage.

**Aerobic fermentation period
(without fermentation trap):** 7 days

**Anaerobic fermentation period
(with fermentation trap):** 4–5 weeks

Colour: Amber

Classification: Table

Minimum storage period: 4–6 months

Fermentation and storage:

During the aerobic fermentation period, stir the fermenting material at least once daily, and keep it at 70°F (21°C). When the period indicated has elapsed, strain off the juice and put it into a clean vessel fitted with a fermentation trap.

During the anaerobic fermentation period, maintain the temperature above 60°F (15·5°C). When bubbling ceases and the froth dies away, rack the wine into a clean, sealed vessel.

Rosehips (top right)
Clover flowers (centre right)
Dandelions (right)
illustrations on pages 82 and 83:
Rose petal wine (above left)
Flowers for making wine (below left)
Elderflower wine (right)

84

Marigold Wine

Main ingredient	**3 quart (3⅗ quart) marigold flower heads**
Other ingredients	**yeast, yeast nutrient rind and juice of 2 lemons**
Water	**1 gallon (1⅕ gallon) water**
Sugar	**3 lb. white sugar**
Additives	**grape tannin, pectin destroying enzyme**

Thoroughly wash the flowers, then boil the water and dissolve the sugar in it. Now put in the flowers, the juice and yellow rind of the lemons, the yeast, the nutrient and the additives; then follow the general instructions for fermentation and storage.

Aerobic fermentation period (without fermentation trap): 7 days

Anaerobic fermentation period (with fermentation trap): 4–6 weeks

Colour: Amber

Classification: Table

Minimum storage period: 6 months

Fermentation and storage:
During the aerobic fermentation period, stir the fermenting material at least once daily, and keep it at 70°F (21°C). When the period indicated has elapsed, strain off the juice and put it into a clean vessel fitted with a fermentation trap.
During the anaerobic fermentation period, maintain the temperature above 60°F (15·5°C). When bubbling ceases and the froth dies away, rack the wine into a clean, sealed vessel.

Rose Hip Wine

Main ingredients	**3 quart (3⅗ quart) ripe rose hips rind and juice of 1 orange**
Other ingredients	**yeast, yeast nutrient**
Water	**1 gallon (1⅕ gallon) water**
Sugar	**2 lb. white sugar**
Additives	**citric acid, grape tannin, pectin destroying enzyme 1 Campden tablet**

Wash and crush the hips with a wooden mallet or heavy spoon. Put them in a deep bowl and pour over the boiling water. Add the rind and juice of the orange, and the crushed Campden tablet. Leave for 24 hours, then stir in the sugar, yeast, nutrient and additives, then follow the general instructions for fermentation and storage.

Aerobic fermentation period (without fermentation trap): 3 days

Anaerobic fermentation period (with fermentation trap): 3 months

Colour: Rosé

Classification: Table

Minimum storage period: 12–18 months

Fermentation and storage:
During the aerobic fermentation period, stir the fermenting material at least once daily, and keep it at 70°F (21°C). When the period indicated has elapsed, strain off the juice and put it into a clean vessel fitted with a fermentation trap.
During the anaerobic fermentation period, maintain the temperature above 60°F (15·5°C). When bubbling ceases and the froth dies away, rack the wine into a clean, sealed vessel.

Rose Petal Wine

Carnation petals can be used in the same way. Again, the old-fashioned, strongly scented white variety are best.

Main ingredients	**2 quart (2⅖ quart) rose petals (red scented roses are best) 1 lemon 6 oz. chopped sultanas 1 orange**
Other ingredients	**yeast, yeast nutrient**
Water	**1 gallon (1⅕ gallon) water**
Sugar	**3 lb. white sugar**
Additives	**citric acid, grape tannin, pectin destroying enzyme**

Put the flower heads in a bowl, pour the boiling water over them, then add the sugar, sultanas and the yellow rind and juice of the orange and lemon. Stir well to dissolve the sugar—when the mixture is lukewarm, add the yeast, nutrient and additives. Then follow the general instructions for fermentation and storage.

Aerobic fermentation period (without fermentation trap): 1 week

Anaerobic fermentation period (with fermentation trap): 4–6 weeks

Colour: White

Classification: Table

Minimum storage period: 6 months to 1 year

Fermentation and storage:
During the aerobic fermentation period, stir the fermenting material at least once daily, and keep it at 70°F (21°C). When the period indicated has elapsed, strain off the juice and put it into a clean vessel fitted with a fermentation trap.

During the anaerobic fermentation period, maintain the temperature above 60°F (15·5°C). When bubbling ceases and the froth dies away, rack the wine into a clean, sealed vessel.

Sloe Wine

Main ingredient	3½ lb. sloes
Other ingredients	yeast, yeast nutrient ½ lb. raisins
Water	1 gallon (1⅕ gallon) water
Sugar	3½ lb. white sugar
Additive	pectin destroying enzyme

Place the sloes in a bowl, and pour enough boiling water over them to cover. Mash them well, then add the raisins (chopped) and sugar dissolved in boiling water to make up the gallon. When cooled to about 70°F (21°C), add the yeast, nutrient and additive. Then follow the general instructions for fermentation and storage.

Aerobic fermentation period (without fermentation trap): 10 days

Anaerobic fermentation period (with fermentation trap): 4 weeks

Colour: Red

Classification: Dessert

Minimum storage period: 1 year

Fermentation and storage:
During the aerobic fermentation period, stir the fermenting material at least once daily, and keep it at 70°F (21°C). When the period indicated has elapsed, strain off the juice and put it into a clean vessel fitted with a fermentation trap.
During the anaerobic fermentation period, maintain the temperature above 60°F (15·5°C). When bubbling ceases and the froth dies away, rack the wine into a clean, sealed vessel.

Barley Wine

Maize can be used in this recipe instead of the barley.

Main ingredients	1 lb. pearl barley 1 lb. chopped raisins 1 large, old potato, sliced 1 orange 1 lemon
Other ingredients	yeast, yeast nutrient
Water	1 gallon (1⅕ gallon) water
Sugar	4 lb. demerara sugar
Additives	citric acid, grape tannin

Put the barley, split raisins, the scrubbed, sliced potato
86

(no need to peel) and sugar into a large bowl, and pour over the boiling water. Peel the orange and lemon thinly; squeeze out the juices. Add the rind and juice to the contents of the bowl, and stir well. Cream the yeast with a little of the liquid and add to the mixture in the bowl, with the additives and nutrient when it has become lukewarm. Then follow the general instructions for fermentation and storage.

Aerobic fermentation period (without fermentation trap): 3–4 weeks

Anaerobic fermentation period (with fermentation trap): 4–6 weeks

Colour: White

Classification: Table

Minimum storage period: 6 months

Fermentation and storage:
During the aerobic fermentation period, stir the fermenting material at least once daily, and keep it at 70°F (21°C). When the period indicated has elapsed, strain off the juice and put it into a clean vessel fitted with a fermentation trap.
During the anaerobic fermentation period, maintain the temperature above 60°F (15·5°C). When bubbling ceases and the froth dies away, rack the wine into a clean, sealed vessel.

Hop Wine

Main ingredient	3 oz. hops
Other ingredients	yeast, yeast nutrient 1 oz. ginger, 1 orange, 1 lemon
Water	1 gallon (1⅕ gallon) water
Sugar	3 lb. white sugar
Additive	citric acid

Boil the hops with the crushed ginger for about one hour, then strain off the liquor into a bowl containing the sugar and juice of the orange and lemon. Add the yeast, nutrient and additive, then follow the general instructions for fermentation and storage; note that there need be no aerobic fermentation period.

Anaerobic fermentation period (with fermentation trap): 4–5 weeks

Colour: White

Classification: Table

Minimum storage period: 6 months

Fermentation and storage:
During the anaerobic fermentation period, maintain the temperature above 60°F (15·5°C). When bubbling ceases and the froth dies away, rack the wine into a clean, sealed vessel.

Methalglyn

Rice Wine

Honey can be used instead of raisins.

Main ingredients	1 lb. (2⅔ cups) crushed rice (wholemeal or 'paddy' rice, *not* polished)
	1 lb. chopped raisins
Other ingredients	yeast, yeast nutrient
	rind and juice of 1 large lemon
Water	1 gallon (1⅕ gallon) water
Sugar	3 lb. white sugar
Additives	citric acid, grape tannin

Pour the boiling water on to the rice, chopped raisins, lemon rind and sugar. Stir well to dissolve the sugar. When cool, add the lemon juice, yeast, nutrient and additives. Then follow the general instructions for fermentation and storage.

Aerobic fermentation period
(without fermentation trap): 7 days

Anaerobic fermentation period
(with fermentation trap): 4–6 weeks

Colour: White

Classification: Table

Minimum storage period: 6–8 months

Fermentation and storage:
During the aerobic fermentation period, stir the fermenting material at least once daily, and keep it at 70°F (21°C). When the period indicated has elapsed, strain off the juice and put it into a clean vessel fitted with a fermentation trap.
During the anaerobic fermentation period, maintain the temperature above 60°F (15·5°C). When bubbling ceases and the froth dies away, rack the wine into a clean, sealed vessel.

Wheat Wine

Main ingredients	1½ lb. wheat
	1 lb. raisins
	1 lb. sultanas
Other ingredients	rind and juice of 1 lemon, 1 orange and 1 grapefruit
	yeast, yeast nutrient
Water	1 gallon (1⅕ gallon) water
Sugar	2½ lb. white sugar
Additive	grape tannin

Crush the wheat in a mincer, chop the dried fruit and add the thinly-pared fruit rinds and sugar. Pour boiling water over the mixture. Stir well and cover until cool. Add fruit juice, nutrient, yeast and additive, then follow the general instructions for fermentation and storage.

Aerobic fermentation period
(without fermentation trap): 7 days

Anaerobic fermentation period
(with fermentation trap): 4–6 weeks

Colour: White

Classification: Table

Minimum storage period: 6 months

Fermentation and storage:
During the aerobic fermentation period, stir the fermenting material at least once daily, and keep it at 70°F (21°C). When the period indicated has elapsed, strain off the juice and put it into a clean vessel fitted with a fermentation trap.
During the anaerobic fermentation period, maintain the temperature above 60°F (15·5°C). When bubbling ceases and the froth dies away, rack the wine into a clean, sealed vessel.

Fortified Wines

The following wines are suitable for fortification with Polish vodka, which is tasteless:
Elderberry Port, Barley Wine, Plum Wine, Apricot Wine, Elderberry Wine, Cherry Port, Rice Wine, Orange Wine, Blackcurrant Wine, Bilberry Wine.
Any Port- or Sherry-type canned grape juice concentrate may also be used. The alcoholic content is raised by 18–20% by volume; the spirit is added after the first racking.

Wine trouble shooting

Fault	Cause	Remedy
Fermentation will not start.	Must too cold.	Raise to 70–75°F (21–24°C).
	Must too hot.	Cool, and add more yeast – overheating kills yeast. Some special yeasts take a week to get going. If nothing happens after a week, either add a teaspoon of granulated baker's yeast, or reduce the sugar concentration by diluting the must with warm water, then add new yeast.
	If Campden tablets used in must, yeast added too soon.	Wait 24 hours, then add fresh yeast.
Fermentation will not stop.		This is not really a fault; the longer fermentation continues the more sugar is being converted to alcohol.
Wine turns acid (vinegar).	Vinegar fly has had access.	Throw the wine away and after sterilization start again. This time make sure the fly cannot penetrate.
Wine too sweet, and alcohol content low.	Too much sugar added initially. Lack of yeast nutrient. Lack of acid.	Blend with a very dry or bitter wine. Use for cooking, punch or sangria. Next time, add the sugar in two spaced portions, add nutrient and citric acid.
Acid wine.	Too much citric acid or other acid fruit.	Add sugar, or glycerine at the rate of 1 teaspoon per bottle.
Yeasty flavour.		Nothing wrong, let the wine mature longer.
'Off' flavours.	Lees allowed to accumulate.	Rack before storage, then every four to eight weeks, according to deposit in storage jar.
Hazy wine.	Pectin haze – pectin not destroyed in fruit wines.	Clear the wine by filtering or finings. Next time, use a pectin-destroying enzyme.
	Starch haze – unripe fruit, especially apples.	Use Bentonite, a very efficient clearing agent.
White wine turning dark colour.	Possibly oxidation.	Further darkening may be prevented by adding 2 Campden tablets, or $\frac{1}{4}$ oz. citric acid per gallon.
Tasteless or insipid wine.	Insufficient citric acid or tannin.	Blend with a harsh or acid wine. Next time, include the recommended additives.

Cider, Mead and Methalglyn

Cider is the pure juice of apples. Similarly, PERRY is the pure juice of pears, using the same method (for 'apples' read 'pears'). Nothing needs to be added until the time of drinking—not even sugar, unless you prefer a sweet cider to a dry one.

Although the ideal type of apple is open to argument, one thing is certain—the apples must be juicy and tart and they must be firm; a mushy apple is no good for cider making. After gathering, the apples should be left out of doors to weather for a while. The best way is to spread them out on racks in the sun.

The apples are then chopped, beaten and crushed in a wooden tub until the juice begins to flow. An enamelled mincer can be used, but nothing metallic must come into contact with the fruit. Put the pulp in a sack—an old pillowcase is just the thing for a small quantity. The sack should not be too tightly packed and the opening must be stitched securely.

Now the juice must be strained through the sack. At this stage, you really need a fruit press, with a screw or a handle for winching the pulp down so that the juice is forced through the tap at the bottom into a receiving vessel. Failing that, an old (but clean) stone sink with an outlet hole is a good substitute. With a flat piece of wood, press out all the juice from the sack of pulp, so that it drains through the plug hole into a bucket underneath. If you are lucky enough to find one, use an old-fashioned mangle with wooden rollers!

When you have extracted all the juice, pour it into a fermentation jar, filling it to just below the top. Plug it with cotton wool which has been dipped in a solution of hot water and one Campden tablet. This will prevent any small flies, especially the vinegar fly, from getting inside the jar. Stand the jar on a tray in a warm place. If the cider froths over the top, clean the neck of the jar and fit a new plug. When frothing has ceased, remove the plug, fit a fementation trap and leave to ferment completely. This will take three to four months. Syphon into bottles without corking tightly.

This method gives a dry cider. If you want a sweet cider, add 4 oz. (½ cup) sugar to each gallon (1⅕ gallon) just prior to drinking. Allow time for the sugar to dissolve, and drink soon after adding it.

Pressing apples for cider (right)

90

Dry Mead

3 lb. honey (creamy-white)
water as required
⅓ pint (⅞ cup) cold weak tea
juice of 1 orange
juice of 1 lemon
½ oz. (4 teaspoons) baker's yeast or mead yeast
yeast nutrient
¼ teaspoon tartaric acid
lumps of sugar

Make the honey up to one gallon (1¼ gallon) with water and bring it to the boil, stirring well (from the bottom of the pan) until the honey has melted and is evenly blended. Simmer for five minutes. Add the cold tea and leave until lukewarm, then add the orange and lemon juice, and sprinkle in the yeast, nutrient and tartaric acid.

Strain through a funnel lined with filter paper or muslin, into a fermentation jar. Plug the neck of the jar with cotton wool and leave for three days, renewing the cotton wool as it becomes soaked with froth and cleaning the neck of the jar. Replace the cotton wool with a fermentation trap; rack off into another jar. Fit a fermentation trap to the second jar, leave in a warm, dark place for two to three months (or until cleared), then rack off into bottles, priming each bottle with a lump of sugar. Cork securely and store for six months before drinking.

The longer mead is kept, the better it is—some believe that no mead is any good until it is 12 months old. It all depends on how strong-minded you are!

Methalglyn

4 lb. thick honey
juice and rind of 1 lemon
8 oz. (2 cups) demerara sugar
4½ pints (11¼ cups) water
½ oz. bruised root ginger
6 cloves
2-inch stick cinnamon
generous grating nutmeg
1 oz. (¼ cup) split raisins
⅓ pint (⅞ cup) cold tea
small packet sherry yeast

Put the honey, rind and juice of the lemon, with the sugar, in the water. Add the bruised root ginger, cloves, cinnamon, nutmeg and raisins, and boil for five to ten minutes; add the cold tea. When the liquid is cool, add the yeast and stir well.

Strain into a fermentation jar. Plug the neck of the jar with cotton wool and leave for three days, removing froth as it rises.

Syphon the methalglyn into a jar fitted with a fermentation trap and leave in a warm, dark place for two to three months, or until cleared. Then rack off into bottles, priming each bottle with a lump of sugar. Cork securely and store for at least six months before drinking. The longer it is kept, the better it tastes.

This is a spiced mead. Serve it at room temperature, as it is not very palatable when served chilled.

An old press for cider-making (right)
Cider as a refreshing summer drink (below)

Making Beer

Introduction

History

The history of beer is long and involved, for its origins can be traced back some 6000 years to Mesopotamia, when a bread mash was fermented with added spices for flavouring. Via the Egyptians, Greeks and Romans, beer eventually arrived in Northern Europe.

The early grain drinks used honey as their source of sugar and were always referred to as ale; the word beer did not come into use until much later but the two names are synonymous. Much of the early ale was brewed from malted wheat, oats and barley; hops were not in common use until introduced by Flemish settlers in the early 16th century.

Recipes from the Middle Ages included elderberry ale, blackberry ale and cowslip ale. These recipes used such ingredients as saltpetre, quassia chips and the roots of many types of vegetables. The main reason for these additives was to mask the considerable number of 'off' flavours.

Beer used to be brewed by every large household, there being a 'brewing day' set aside once a week. The beers produced were much stronger than our present-day commercial beers and were brewed in large quantities in oak casks.

Around the 1780s beer began to be produced on a commercial scale by small breweries. The excellent beers they produced were delivered by brewer's dray to within a few miles of the brewery. Gradually, linked with the vast increase in population and improved transport, breweries amalgamated and the many small local breweries were replaced by fewer, much larger establishments, producing fewer types of beer.

Summarized Theory

Beer is made from a mixture of malted grain, water, sugar, yeast and hops. The basic process is as follows. Grain, usually barley, is malted, that is to say, the grains are spread out in a malt house under controlled conditions of moisture and temperature. Just after sprouting, the starch in the grain is converted into the fermentable sugar called maltose. The grain is now dried in a kiln to inhibit further growth, and stored until required. The malted and dried grain is boiled with water in a large container and the liquor—the wort—is strained off the mash. Sugar and yeast are added, fermentation commences and the sugar is gradually converted to alcohol. At the end of the fermentation process the beer is filtered and put into containers.

For home brewing it is usual, and easier, to use concentrated liquid malt extract to which a little grain malt and fresh hops may be added. The concentrate gives body to the beer while the other ingredients add colour, maltiness and hop flavour.

A certain amount of sugar added to each gallon gives added strength. As a general guide, a strong beer or stout needs about 2 lb. of total sugar content (i.e. malt

An engraving after Hogarth's 'Beer Street' (right)

extract plus sugar) per gallon, while a weaker beer needs 1 lb. per gallon.

Water, or liquor as it is known in the brewing industry, has an important role to play in the particular style of beer. Particular types of water produce unique beers. As a general guide, soft water areas produce good brown ales and stouts, and hard water areas produce the bitter beers.

The hop is a vine-like climbing plant from which the beer obtains its characteristic bitterness. The hop adds resins, which give the beer its bitterness, and essential oils which give the 'hoppy' aroma to the beer.

Yeast is at the heart of all fermentation. It is a single-celled organism that requires sugar and vitamin B, in addition to several acids and ammonium salts in various degrees, in which to flourish. Fortunately, malt wort is an ideal medium in which yeast can grow and multiply. The great danger to the brewer is that wild yeasts abound in the atmosphere and infection from such yeasts can have damaging effects.

Beer Classification

The number of breweries in existence produce differing flavours and textures of beer to suit the varied tastes of beer drinkers. The main categories of home brewed beers are as follows.

Bitter this is well hopped, with a fairly strong alcohol content. The commencing gravity would be in the region of 1·045–1·050. The beer may vary in colour and flavour, but should have an underlying residual bitterness.

Pale ale sometimes called *Light ale*. A bitter beer similar in style to a *Dinner ale* with a starting gravity of about 1·030. This beer should be clean and light on the palate and not too 'hoppy' in flavour.

Indian pale ale a bitter beer, with more hops in the flavour than light ale; it has a starting gravity of around 1·040. Fuller-bodied than light ale, with a malty flavour. This beer should be well balanced and clean on the palate.

Brown ale home brewed brown ale is one of the most individual ales produced. The colour can range from amber to a very dark brown. The degree of sweetness can vary but there should be an underlying residual sweetness, gained by the addition of lactose. Brown beer is lightly hopped.

Irish stout a dark drink with a full flavour and characteristic bitterness underlying the flavour. Irish stout should have a creamy, close-knit head.

Sweet, or milk, stout dark and sweet, but still with an underlying bitter tang.

Oatmeal stout not as bitter as Irish stouts or as sweet as a sweet stout; a special flavour is imparted by the oatmeal.

Barley wine this is a heavy, sweet beer, with a high alcohol content. It is full-flavoured, but slightly more bitter than would normally be expected from a brown beer. The starting gravity is often of the order of 1·080.

Lager this is a light-bodied and light-coloured beer with a very delicate hop flavour. A fairly high starting gravity of 1·050 is essential. A lager yeast (bottom fermenting) should always be used, but lager is not easy for the amateur to imitate. The nearest amateur approach is a light-flavoured, light ale style, with a higher alcohol content. A continental hop (such as Hallertau or Saar) should be used.

Typical Compositions and Gravities of Commercial Beers

Type	Malt barley per gallon	Hops in ounces per gallon	Starting specific gravity	Approximate alcohol content
Pale Ale	2 lb.	$\frac{3}{4}$–1	1·055	6%
	1 lb. 12 oz.	$\frac{1}{2}$–$\frac{3}{4}$	1·048	5%
	1$\frac{1}{2}$ lb.	$\frac{1}{4}$–$\frac{1}{2}$	1·040	4$\frac{1}{4}$%
Light Ale	1 lb. 2 oz.	$\frac{3}{4}$	1·032	3$\frac{1}{2}$%
	1$\frac{1}{4}$ lb.		1·035	
Strong Ale	2$\frac{1}{2}$ lb.	1–2	1·070	8%
Stout	1$\frac{1}{4}$ lb.	$\frac{1}{2}$–$\frac{3}{4}$	1·035	3$\frac{1}{2}$–4$\frac{1}{2}$%
	1 lb. 10 oz.		1·045	
Lager (Pilsener type)	2 lb.	$\frac{1}{2}$	1·045	6%

Beer Packs

Beer packs contain sufficient ingredients and instructions to make a given quantity of beer and are aimed at the person who prefers not to experiment in brewing. It is a matter of trial and error to establish which type of kit gives best value.

One of the difficulties in using beer packs is to ensure that the beer has a good close-knit head and, more important, has the ability to retain this head. To avoid difficulty in fermentation, make sure that you boil your ingredients in water and allow them to cool before adding your yeast. A further tip is to buy a beer pack in which the yeast included is a top fermenting yeast.

Hops (left)
The drawing, A, on the far left shows the flowers or cones of the hop plant. It is the ripened cones of the female plant which impart the characteristic bitter flavour to malt liquor such as beers and ales. The other drawing, B, shows the long stalk of the plant twined around the hop pole

Ingredients and Equipment

Ingredients

Water A chemist can give advice as to the correct chemicals to add to your local water supply to produce the desired standard of hard or soft water, but a useful guide for adjustment of the water for different beers is to add one teaspoon of ordinary table salt to each full gallon in hard water areas to facilitate production of browns and stouts. In soft water areas, one level teaspoon of magnesium sulphate to each full gallon of brew assists in brewing bitters and pale ales.

The type of liquor is more important to beer made from grain mashes than to malt extract brews.

Sugar For the home brewer, refined granulated sugar is as good as any and is one hundred percent pure. For making brown beers or stouts, it is quite safe to use small quantities of brown sugar. When deciding the amount of sugar to be added to your grains, or grist, for mashing beers add about 15% by weight for pale beers and a little more for browns and stouts.

Lactose is a form of milk sugar and is unfermentable by brewer's yeast. Home brewers use it to sweeten their brown beers and stouts.

Malt extract Wort, the infusion of malt extracted from the barley, is evaporated into a syrup; it is highly fermentable. There are one or two malt extracts that are specially produced to contain a proportion of dextrins which give beer more body and better head retention.

If the beer has been made from malt extracts only, there will be very little deposit apart from the copious yeast lees and it is possible to rack off nearly all the beer into a container.

Malt extract may be hopped or unhopped. If you use hopped extract it saves the task of boiling up fresh hops.

Hops Many of the essential oils contained in hops are lost in the boiling so that some experts advocate retaining up to a third of the hops until the last quarter hour of the boiling. Others suggest adding a few hops either just prior to pitching the yeast or during storage in the cask at the end of the brew. This is a matter of personal preference. The tannin found in the hops has a dual role in that it helps to prevent bacterial infection of the beer, and also assists in its eventual clarification.

It is difficult for the layman to identify good hops from poor ones. There are, however, a few pointers. The smell should be clean and should have no cheese odour; the colour should be pale green or golden dependent on the type of hop. Beware of hops that have an excess of brown leaves, for this indicates that they are old and oxidised. If hops are bought in bulk, ensure that the storage space is cool and dry.

Yeast Contamination by wild yeasts can be avoided by the addition of an active yeast starter to the wort as soon as it is cool enough: 58°–60°F (14·5°–15·5°C). A golden rule in the use of yeast is to make sure you have a true strain of beer yeast. Never use a baker's or wine yeast, or the beer will lack quality and the yeast will not settle hard on the bottom of the bottle.

Glasses for serving wine and beer (right)

Two types of yeast are in general use by the home brewer. Top fermenting yeast 'works' or ferments best at a temperature of around 58°–60°F (14·5°–15·5°C) and it must be emphasized that every effort should be made to keep your wort down to this figure, to avoid 'yeast bite', which will give your beer an acrid bitterness. A vigorous, rousing stirring will help the fermentation. This is especially important when fermenting out the high gravity beers, in particular the barley wines.

The second type of yeast normally used is the bottom fermented type. This is used in the brewing of continental-type lager, which is fermented for a much longer period and at a temperature as low as 39°–45°F (4·0°–7·2°C).

To recapitulate, use only authentic top fermenting yeasts for bitter beers, browns and stouts. For lagers use the continental bottom fermenting lager yeasts. It is possible to skim off some of your yeast from the top of your wort to re-use on your next brew, but be very careful. Store the yeast in your refrigerator but not for longer than one week; do not allow it to freeze. This, of course, does not apply to yeast purchased in sealed packets or bottles which will, of course, last for many months if stored correctly, although once opened, the contents must be used immediately. Never use a baker's yeast or a wine yeast to make beer.

Primary Equipment

The most important utensil is a large mashing vessel. This can range from a large one gallon saucepan to a small domestic boiler. The larger the vessel the easier it is to make a large quantity of beer at any one time. It is much easier to mash your grist if you have gas as a heat source, for with electricity, once you have the required heat for your liquor, it is difficult to switch off instantly and then to reheat quickly.

The next most important item is a large, immersible thermometer to check the mashing temperature. About 12 inches in length is ideal, larger if you wish, but certainly no smaller. As a safety precaution, it is a good idea to have a spare thermometer handy.

A plastic dustbin or large pail, with a well fitting lid and lifting handles, is used to ferment the brew after the yeast has been added. A vessel of about five gallons capacity is necessary, and if it has a smooth interior surface it will be easier to clean.

A flexible $\frac{1}{4}$ inch plastic tube, about three feet in length, is used for syphoning off the beer into bottles or a cask. Ideally it can be fitted with a glass syphon tube with a 'U' bend, to prevent the sediment from being drawn up. A small plastic tap or even a clothes peg on the other end makes it easier to fill bottles to a required level and stop the flow quickly and easily.

All bottles used must be in good condition and must not be cracked or chipped. The large two pint size is ideal, and are better still if they have screw tops. Ordinary half pint or one pint beer bottles are excellent,

Some ingredients and equipment for making beer

but you will require a considerable number. To close them a crown cork is easily fixed by a small hand crowner.

A bottle brush is necessary to clean thoroughly the insides of the bottles.

Optional Equipment

A large, fine mesh strainer is a great advantage, a useful size being at least 10 inches in diameter and six inches deep, although a larger size is better still.

A tough plastic or glass measuring jug is useful, with graduations of weight and fluid capacity marked on the side. Once you have weighed a quantity of malt extract, grain or sugar you can note the mark on your jug and are always sure of measuring a consistent amount.

The specific gravity is measured with a hydrometer covering the range 1·000–1·300. A trial jar, which is used to contain the liquid in which the hydrometer floats, should be purchased at the same time.

A plastic funnel can be used to fill bottles with primings or finings at the end of the process.

Self-adhesive labels are useful for labelling bottles before storage—it is easy to forget their contents after a few weeks. Write on the labels the quantities of all the ingredients, the appropriate date, and other relevant information. If you copy these labels into a book you will have a complete record of your brewing activities and an opportunity to repeat or amend a brew on a subsequent occasion.

Hygiene

Basically the same requirements as for wine making apply, as cleanliness is half the battle in home brewing. In every house there are scores of minute wild yeast spores present. The best way to sterilize your equipment is to use Campden tablets. These tablets contain sodium metabisulphate, which, when dissolved, produces sulphur dioxide—a powerful sterilizer. Two ounces in a pint of cool water is a good strength to use. It is a good idea to make up a stock solution for general use.

After a piece of equipment has been liberally swilled in this solution, drain it off and allow it to stand for a few minutes before use. This allows the sulphur dioxide to evaporate, leaving the surface sterilized. You can usually use the same solution two or three times before discarding it.

A hop garden

Basic techniques

Preparing the Wort
Preparation of malt extract and adding sugar

This procedure applies to most of the basic beer recipes which follow; variations from this procedure are described in the recipes. Warm the contents of a can of concentrated malt extract by opening the can and standing it in hot water for about ten minutes. This makes it easier to pour. Pour the extract into a saucepan and mix in any additives (crystal malt, black malt or colouring) required by the recipe.

Add one pint (2½ cups) of boiling water for each pound of extract. Stir the mixture to achieve an even consistency and gently bring to the boil, then boil vigorously for about five minutes. The more vigorous the boil the better the results.

Place the measured quantity of sugar into a well-cleaned fermenting vessel and pour in the contents of the saucepan, stirring well.

If you are using a concentrated hopped malt extract you can now proceed with the fermentation stage. If however you are using an unhopped extract you should place a lid on the fermenting vessel and begin to prepare the grain malt and hops.

Adding grain malt and hops

If you are using grain malts, these should first be crushed. This is most easily done by placing them on and covering them with a cloth, then rolling a rolling pin over them. They should be just crushed with the husk still visible in flakes.

Weigh out or measure the crushed grain malt and hops, retaining one third of the hops for the final boiling.

A useful tip at this stage is to place the crushed malt and hops in a clean muslin or mutton cloth bag, to prevent the mixture from sticking to the bottom of the saucepan. Place the bag in a saucepan and add the required quantity of hot water.

Cover the saucepan and bring the mixture to the boil, then simmer for 45 minutes, adding the final third of the hops after 30 minutes. Pour the contents through a fine strainer on to the malt extract solution in the fermenting vessel.

Fermentation

Make up the beer wort to the required volume by adding cool water (to replace any that may have evaporated), checking that the temperature of the wort is about 60°F (15°C). Pitch in the yeast, sprinkling it over the surface of the mixture, and stir well. The addition of a teaspoon of yeast energizer is advantageous.

Place the lid on the fermenting vessel and leave in a warm, even temperature. During the first 24 hours, stir the wort vigorously five or six times; a frothy, white head should form. As it starts to settle, skim off the early yeast and waste using a wooden spoon.

The duration of fermentation will depend on room temperature: the warmer the temperature the more quickly the beer will ferment.

1. *Warming the can of malt extract*

2. *Pouring the warmed malt extract into a pan*

3. *Adding the boiled extract and water to the sugar*

4. *Cracking the grain*

5. *Adding hops to the grain*

6. *Straining grain and hops onto malt extract solution*

The following figures may be a useful guide.

75°F (24°C) — four days
60°F (15°C) — five days
50°F (10°C) — ten days

After skimming, give the wort a final stir and allow it to attenuate, or lower its specific gravity by continued fermentation towards the final specific gravity of 1·000. Prior to the end of the attenuation period (at a specific gravity of about 1·006), the brew may be strained off into one gallon jars and sealed with an airlock; this precaution precludes the contamination of the brew by bacterial infection.

Filtering and Storage

When measuring the specific gravity, take sufficient liquid out of the brew and fill a trial jar to the brim. Blow off any surface bubbles and lower the hydrometer

7. *Adding cool water to the beer wort*

8. *Sprinkling on dried yeast to start fermentation*
108

9. *Skimming off the early yeast*

(twisting it gently to allow any air bubbles adhering to it to escape). Read the indication.

Once in the gallon jars the brew is left to attenuate to the final gravity, then when the fermentation stops, allowed to stand for a couple of days in a cool place for the sediment to settle. Then syphon off the beer from the lees, aiming for as little yeast deposit remaining as possible.

If the brew is not clear after this first syphoning, add a small quantity of an isinglass-based beer finings. Return the brew with the added finings to the gallon jars (which should be re-sterilized while empty), and replace the airlock. The jars should then be left in a cool place for five to ten days and then the syphoning process repeated. Make sure that you have sufficient bottles and stoppers or caps, and that they are all completely sterile.

Obtain a glass tube with the end bent up into a 'U' (or hook) about ½ inch long, and insert the long arm into a plastic tube. If available, fit a plastic tap to the other end of the tube. Gently lower the U-shaped end of the

10. *Checking the specific gravity in a trial jar*

glass tube into the beer.

A useful technique when syphoning is to position the jar about one foot higher than the top of the bottle to be used.

Turn on the tap and suck the end of the tube until the beer flows. To stop the flow, turn off the tap or clamp the tube with a clothes peg. Alternatively, use a syphon-pump as in wine making.

Partly fill your bottles with the brew. Add one teaspoon of priming sugar (this should preferably be made from one pound of sugar, boiled in half a pint of water until dissolved and allow to cool) to each partly-filled bottle. The priming sugar is added to give the yeast some sugar from which to create the carbon dioxide required to make the beer gaseous.

Fill the bottle to within about an inch of the bottom of the closure, then secure the closure tightly. Label each bottle and note the date and type of brew. Turn the bottles upside down and check for leaks.

Store the bottles in a warm place for a few days until

13. Syphoning the beer into the primed bottles

11. Adding finings to the beer

14. Tapping on crown corks

12. Priming the bottles with sugar

the secondary fermentation is complete and the beer is gassy. After ten days (lagers, three weeks), release the closure on one of the bottles; if gas escapes, reseal immediately. The brew is ready for storage.

If you have the space available, the flavour, condition and head retention of the beer is greatly improved by storing the beer in a cool place for two or three months. Storing the beer for longer periods does not improve the flavour, but neither does the beer deteriorate.

The production of draught beer is an alternative to producing bottled beer. Useful containers are the larger plastic, wine or sherry containers at present available. These should, of course, be thoroughly sterilized and must be able to withstand slight internal pressures. Simply rack off the beer into the container as if it were a large bottle, prime at the normal rate and screw the tap well in. The advantage of this type of container is the time saved in bottling and washing. The beer should keep well for up to three weeks.

109

Serving

Beers containing sediment tend to cloud when opened, this being caused by the sediment being carried to the top by rising carbon dioxide. A large bottle is often better poured straight into a jug before serving in individual glasses. If the beer is a little lively, keep the bottle in a refrigerator for a day to lessen activity.

Open the bottle, hold it midway along its length and gently lower the top to the edge of the glass, which should be held at an angle. The beer will then run down the side into the glass. Gently pivot the bottom of the glass until the glass is in the vertical position and gently raise the bottom of the bottle, towards the horizontal. Take care not to return the bottle to an upright position until you have finished pouring, or the sediment will rise, clouding the beer. If you are going to fill several glasses from a large bottle, retain the bottle in a near horizontal position as you move from glass to glass.

Incidentally, the rather cloudy, small amount of beer left in the bottom of the bottle is very rich in vitamin B. It is very beneficial to drink or you can use it as a yeast to ferment your next brew, by mixing it into the wort. Indeed, once you start brewing regularly you can re-use the same yeast, changing it, say, every third brew.

Beer Recipes

Reminders

The brewer who makes beer from malt extract must exercise rigorous temperature control. If malt is dried at too high a temperature the enzymes will react inefficiently and the beer will be low in sugar. A further temperature to watch is that of the water used in the extracting process, which must not be too hot.

For simplification, in the following basic beer recipes, the same quantity (4 lb.) of unhopped, concentrated liquid malt extract has been used throughout. To avoid boiling the hops initially, you can use a hopped malt extract and, of course, can then omit the quantity of hops given in the recipes. Both hopped and unhopped types are usually supplied in cans; a light-coloured or pale extract should be obtained. You can use this same extract for all the recipes, simply varying the quantities of sugar, hops, grain, malts and water to give the different beers, as directed.

As you gain confidence and develop a preference for certain types of beer, you will naturally wish to experiment and brew to suit your own palate. To vary the bitterness of the beers, slightly increase or decrease the quantity of hops. A $\frac{1}{4}$ oz. variance per gallon either way, will normally be noticeable and provide a yardstick for adjusting the flavour next time.

Some more unusual recipes follow the conventional beer recipes.

Some ingredients for making beer (right)

112

Best Bitter

4 gallons ($4\frac{4}{5}$ gallons) water
4 lb. unhopped light malt extract
2 lb. sugar
1 lb. cracked crystal malt
4 oz. hops
$\frac{1}{2}$ oz. dried yeast

Variations from basic method None

Description
This is a bitter beer, of which the colour and taste can vary, but there must be an underlying bitterness of taste. This recipe produces a brew with a starting specific gravity of 1·045 and an alcohol content of 4·4%.

Light Ale

5 gallons (6 gallons) water
$1\frac{3}{4}$ lb. brown malt
$1\frac{1}{2}$ oz. crushed barley
$1\frac{1}{2}$ lb. brown sugar
3 oz. hops
yeast brew

Variations from basic method
Boil the hops, malt and barley for 30 minutes, strain on to the sugar and allow to cool until lukewarm, then add the yeast brew. Cover and allow to ferment for about 48 hours, until the specific gravity decreases to 1·008. Bottle without disturbing the sediment. The beer can be drunk after five days, but improves with storage.

Description
In this example the beer is not primed but racked and bottled while there is still some sugar present. The beer produced is dry and effervescent during storage in the bottle. The final product should be lighter in flavour, strength and bitterness than bitter beer. The starting specific gravity should be 1·030 with an alcohol content of 3·7%.

Brown Ale

4 gallons ($4\frac{4}{5}$ gallons) water
4 lb. unhopped light malt extract
2 lb. sugar
$\frac{3}{4}$ lb. cracked crystal malt
$\frac{1}{4}$ lb. cracked roast barley or black malt
3 oz. hops
$\frac{1}{2}$ oz. dried yeast

Variations from basic method None

Description
This is a sweet beer and the colour can range from amber to dark brown. The degree of sweetness can vary but there should be an underlying residual sweetness. The starting gravity should be 1·045 and there should be an alcohol content of about 5%.

Strong Ale

3 gallons ($3\frac{3}{5}$ gallons) water
4 lb. unhopped light malt extract
$\frac{3}{4}$ lb. cracked crystal malt
1 lb. sugar
2 oz. hops
$\frac{1}{2}$ oz. dried yeast

Variations from basic method
The fermentation time for this type of beer is slightly longer than that for normal bitter beer.

Description
This is a beer somewhere between a normal bitter and a barley wine, with a starting gravity of 1·050 and an alcohol content of 6·5%.

Stout

3 gallons ($3\frac{3}{5}$ gallons) water
4 lb. unhopped light malt extract
$\frac{1}{4}$ lb. cracked crystal malt
$\frac{1}{2}$ lb. cracked roasted barley or black malt
1 lb. sugar
3 oz. hops
$\frac{1}{2}$ oz. dried yeast

Variations from basic method None

Description
This beer is heavier in fullness and flavour than brown ale, but still with an underlying sweetness. The starting gravity is around 1·050 and an alcohol content of around 5·8% is typical.

Lager

4 gallons ($4\frac{4}{5}$ gallons) water
4 lb. unhopped light malt extract
$\frac{1}{4}$ lb. cracked crystal malt
2 lb. sugar
3 oz. hops
$\frac{1}{2}$ oz. dried yeast

2 gallons ($2\frac{2}{5}$ gallons) water
4 lb. unhopped light malt extract
$\frac{1}{4}$ lb. cracked crystal malt
1 lb. sugar
2 oz. hops
$\frac{1}{4}$ oz. dried yeast

Variations from basic method
It is too complicated for the amateur to mash using the continental system (called 'decoction'). Instead, follow the basic method and ferment out at a very low temperature, between 45° and 50°F (8° and 10°C). Boil clear and bottle normally.

Hop picking (Harpers, 1885)

Description

This is a light-bodied and pale-coloured beer, with a delicate hop flavour. A bottom-fermenting lager yeast is essential and, where possible, continental hops. This method produces a starting gravity of 1·044 and an alcohol content of 5·8%.

The second recipe is for a typical export lager, which is slightly stronger than normal lager, with a higher starting gravity of 1·045 and an alcohol content around 6%.

Tonic Stout

2 gallons (2⅖ gallons) water
6 lb. parsnips
½ lb. malt extract
4 lb. brown sugar
½ oz. dried yeast
1 teaspoon yeast nutrient
2 tablespoons (2½T) lemon juice

Variations from basic method
Make up a starter bottle with the yeast, a teaspoon of sugar, nutrient, and lemon juice.

Clean the parsnips, but do not peel them; cut them into fairly thick slices. Place half the quantity in your pan and add 4 pints (10 cups) hot water; bring to the boil and simmer for 20 minutes. Pour into the sugar and malt extract in the fermenting vessel, stirring well. Boil up the remaining parsnips in 4 pints (10 cups) water and add to the fermenting vessel. Make up to two gallons (2⅖ gallons) with cold water, adding your starter bottle when the temperature is 60°–70°F (15°–21°C). Ferment, rack, and bottle but do not prime.

Description
This is a rarely-made 'special' beer (technically not a beer if judged by the absence of hops), highly individual in character. An alcohol content in the order of 4–6% should be expected.

Barley Wine

2 gallons (2⅖ gallons) water
4 lb. unhopped malt extract
½ lb. cracked crystal malt
1 lb. sugar
1½ oz. hops
¼ oz. dried yeast

Variations from basic method
Fermentation will be long and slow and the wort will require frequent agitation to prevent the specific gravity from falling.

Some ingredients for tonic stout (above)

illustrations on pages 116 and 117:
Oasthouses for drying hops (above left)
Lager with stout, brown ale and light ale (below left)
Home-brewed beer (right)

Description

This is a heavy, sweet beer, very high in alcohol; it is full-flavoured but slightly more bitter than would be expected of a brown beer. A starting gravity of 1·070 is normal and the beer produced should have an alcohol content of around 7%. This is a strong beer and should be drunk in small quantities and with caution.

Mead Ale

2 gallons (2⅖ gallons) water
3 lb. honey
1 lb. brown (demerera) sugar
½ teaspoon citric acid
1 teaspoon burnt caramel
1½ oz. hops
½ oz. dried yeast
colouring agent (gravy browning)

Variations from basic method

Melt the honey in two pints (5 cups) hot water, and bring to the boil. Add the sugar and simmer for 15 minutes, stirring occasionally, removing the frothy residue as it rises to the surface. Stir in the hops, and simmer for a further 15 minutes before adding another pint (2½ cups) water. Allow the brew to cool until it is lukewarm, then add the citric acid.

Pour the mixture into a well cleaned fermenting vessel and make up to 2 gallons (2⅖ gallons) with cool water, until the temperature is about 60°–70°F (15°–21°C). Add the dried yeast, yeast nutrient and colouring. Ferment, prime and bottle.

Description

There are several varieties of mead ale which depend for their differences on varying alcohol content and the different proportions of the ingredients (especially the honey) used. Mead is a comparatively sweet beer with a smooth body and an alcohol content of 4–6%.

Cider Ale

1 gallon (1⅕ gallon) apple juice
1 teaspoon sugar
½ oz. champagne wine yeast
½ oz. nutrient

Variations from basic method

Make up a starter bottle with the yeast, a teaspoon of sugar, nutrient and 2 tablespoons (2½ T) of the apple juice.

Pour the remainder of the apple juice into a 1 gallon (1⅕ gallon) fermenting jar. Add the contents of the starter bottle and fit a bored cork or rubber bung. Fit a fermentation trap and leave in an even temperature (60°–70°F, 15°–21°C) until all fermentation has ceased and the cider is clear.

Rack, prime, and bottle; leave to mature in cool conditions for about 4 weeks.

Description

This is a dry, light beer, with a characteristic sparkle; the alcohol content is approximately 4–6%.

Ginger Beer

2 gallons (2⅖ gallons) water
1½ lb. sugar (see below)
2 lemons
1 oz. bruised root ginger
½ oz. cream of tartar
½ oz. dried yeast
1 slice toast

Variations from basic method

Peel off the lemon rind and discard it; squeeze the juice into your fermenting vessel, then add the sugar, cream of tartar, and bruised root ginger. Pour 6 pints (15 cups) boiling water on to the ingredients, stirring well. Make up to 2 gallons (2⅖ gallons) with cool water. When it has cooled to 60°–70°F (15°–21°C), take a little of the mixture in a teacup and cream in the yeast. Float the piece of toast on top of the liquid in the fermenting vessel and pour the yeast mixture on to it.

Ferment for 24 hours at an even temperature (60°–70°F, 15°–21°C) before skimming and bottling, using a fine strainer. It will be ready for drinking in 3 days. Check the corks and release any excessive pressure build-up in the first 2 days.

If difficulty is experienced using this recipe, due to insufficient yeast food and the consequent creation of an over-sweet taste, add about one pound of raisins and decrease the amount of sugar by about half.

Description

This is technically not a beer if judged by the absence of hops—it is slightly alcoholic, at approximately 2%. Nevertheless, by taste and the fact that it has a head, it is more nearly a beer than a wine.

Lemon Ginger Beer

2 gallons (2⅖ gallons) water
3 lb. sugar
3 lemons
2 oz. cream of tartar
2 oz. slightly bruised ginger
½ oz. dried yeast

Variations from basic method

Proceed as for Ginger Beer, but place the peeled rind with the juice, ginger, and cream of tartar in the fermenting vessel, before adding the 6 pints (15 cups) boiling water.

Description

Obviously, this is very similar to Ginger Beer, is also only slightly alcoholic, and suits those who prefer a sharper taste.

Nettle Beer

2 gallons (2⅖ gallons) water
fresh, young nettles
1 lb. sugar
½ oz. bruised root ginger
1 lemon, sliced
½ oz. cream of tartar
1 oz. hops
½ oz. dried yeast

Variations from basic method

Place the hops, bruised root ginger and lemon in a pan. Add as many washed nettles as possible, and top up to the brim with hot water. Bring to the boil and simmer for 15 minutes. Place the sugar and cream of tartar in a well-cleaned fermenting vessel and pour the liquid through a strainer into the vessel. Now place any remaining nettles in the pan, top up with hot water, bring to the boil and then simmer for 15 minutes. Strain the brew on to the mixture in the fermenting vessel.

Make up to 2 gallons (2⅖ gallons) with cool water and add the dried yeast at 60°–70°F (15°–21°C). Ferment, skimming off any excess froth as necessary. Rack and bottle; no priming or finings are necessary and the beer can be drunk immediately.

Description

A medium taste beer with a 4–6% alcohol content, Nettle Beer bears a noticeable resemblance to light ale.

Beer makes a refreshing drink (below)

Equipment for making beer (right)

Beer trouble shooting

Fault	Cause	Remedy
Set mash.	Grist crushed too finely, possibly from excessive use of electric grinder.	Dilute by adding water; if this fails, discard.
	Poor quality malted barley.	Add up to 10% of a highly diastatic malt extract (see labels).
Fermentation does not start.	Environment too cold.	Remove to a temperature of at least 60°F (15°C).
	Poor or impoverished yeast.	See Slow Fermentation.
	Specific gravity too high.	Warm the brew, stir vigorously and add yeast.
Slow fermentation	Poor, impoverished or worn-out yeast.	Use a fresh yeast every third brew, of correct type (i.e. not baker's or wine type). Use a yeast starter to give a good initial impetus.
	Poor quality malted barley.	Add yeast nutrient.
	Wort out of balance (excessive dextrins).	Discard.
	Excessive nitrate in water (maximum 5 grains per gallon).	Use normal tap water.
	Fermentation or attenuation temperature too low.	Move to even temperature of 60°F (15°C) – lower temperature permissible for lager.
	Hop content too high (lack of usual 'yeasty' head).	Stir vigorously.
Flat beer (no life).	Faulty bottle closures.	Check sealing rings/corks and rectify.
	Fermentation or attenuation temperature too low.	Next time, maintain temperature of at least 60°F (15°C).
	Interval between fermentation/bottling too long.	Shorten interval.
Sour taste	See Flat Beer.	
	Inefficient sterilizing.	Take more care, using Campden tablets.
	Yeast killed by extreme temperature – above 85°F (29°C) or below 32°F (0°C).	Maintain better temperature control.
Too bitter.	Excessive hops.	Reduce hop content.
	Insufficient air during fermentation.	Remove fermentation cover daily and skim to clear.

Fault	Cause	Remedy
Too sweet.	Excess of malt.	Add $\frac{1}{2}$ teaspoon from starter bottle.
	Insufficient attenuation (specific gravity below 1·010).	Discard.
Too lively.	Specific gravity too high when bottled.	Add $\frac{1}{2}$ teaspoon from starter bottle; don't seal too tightly and release gas daily.
	Excessive use of priming sugar.	Decant into large covered container; avoid contamination.
	Stored at too high a temperature.	Remove to a temperature of 50–55°F (10–13°C).
Yeast bite (intense, acrid bitterness).	Excess of yeast.	Remove yeast and waste matter from periphery of fermentation vessel, with a damp cloth.
	Yeast still in suspension.	Add more finings.
	Storage at too high a temperature (causes sediment to rise and disperse).	Remove to cooler environment.
Insufficient head.	Faulty malt.	Discard.
	Maturation time too short.	Pour into large, covered container; sparingly use starter bottle. Leave in a warmer environment.
	Lack of dextrins.	Mash at a minimum temperature of 152°F (66°C).
	Glasses washed in detergent and not thoroughly rinsed, or dirty.	Clean again and rinse thoroughly.
'Off' flavours	Decomposition of dead yeast cells (autolysis).	Remove by racking.
Cloudy beer.	Storage at too high a temperature.	Remove to cooler environment.
	Insufficient sieving of hops and grain malt.	Add finings.
	Excessive use of finings (saturation).	Discard.
	Too little finings.	Add finings, carefully.
	Filtering too early or ineffective.	Filter again.

Punches, Cups and Mulled Wines

Under this heading there are two rough divisions, Summer coolers and Winter warmers; both have a wine basis and are intended as party or family drinks. The recipes are all easy to prepare, usually taking only a few minutes.

If you have no punch-bowl, a soup tureen and server is a good substitute, or indeed any bowl with a fitted lid to keep in the aroma and flavour.

Briefly, punch is a drink made with hot water mixed with wines or spirits, sweetened and flavoured with spices, lemon or orange. Fruits of your own choice can be added, and one of the secrets of good Old English Punch is the added zest of Seville oranges, lemons or limes (or all three). Lumps of sugar are rubbed against the skin of the fruit until they have absorbed all the fruit's essential oils. The sugar is then added to the punch along with the grated zest.

The potency of your punch varies according to the amount of wine or spirits you put into it. Any kind of red or white wine can be used, and home-made wines are excellent for the purpose. For variety float on top of your cold punch pieces of apples and oranges, soft seasonal berry fruits, herbs such as mint and borage, slices of cucumber, strips of melon, orange and lemon peel.

A word of warning—when heating up wine or cider do not overheat or else the alcohol will evaporate. Heat just enough to make a good warming drink.

Bishop's nightcap (above right)
Planter's punch (right)
A selection of punches (far right)

Summer Punch

4 bottles light ale
½ bottle dry sherry
1 lemon
2 oz. castor (superfine) sugar

Place sugar in punch bowl then pare the lemon rind very thinly and mix in with the sugar. Squeeze the lemon juice into the bowl, let stand for 30 minutes then remove the rind. Then add the ale, sherry and some ice cubes. Sliced lemon or oranges or bunches of cherries will decorate the bowl.

Classification Summer cooler

Apple Punch

A tot of whisky added to each serving in a tall glass makes this more interesting.

1 pint (2½ cups) ginger beer
3 bottles apple wine
2 pints (5 cups) lemonade
fresh orange slices for garnish

Add the ginger beer to the apple wine, place in the ice cube tray and put in the refrigerator. When the ice cubes are frozen, put them in a jug and add the lemonade. Garnish with thin slices of orange.

Classification Summer cooler

Apricot Punch

1 large can apricots
¼ pint (⅝ cup) lemon squash
1 bottle apricot wine
3 bottles sparkling lemonade
slices of lemon
ice
a little soda water

Strain the syrup from the apricots and put the fruit in a large bowl. Pulp them, then add the syrup. Add the lemon squash and, when nearly ready to serve, the wine and lemonade. Float the lemon slices on top and put in ice cubes. To serve, fill the glasses two thirds full and top up with soda water.

Classification Summer cooler

Peach Punch

This drink looks attractive served in tall glasses with a slice or two of peach in each glass and a slice of cucumber fixed to the rim.

1 small can sliced peaches
ice cubes or crushed ice
2 bottles red wine (vin ordinaire)
¾ pint (1⅞ cups) orange squash
¾ pint (1⅞ cups) soda water
sliced cucumber

Drain the peaches and put the juice in a mixing bowl. Add several cubes of ice. Pour in the wine and the squashes, stir well and add the sliced peaches. Put the punch into a serving jug and, just before serving, add the soda water and float sliced cucumber on top.

Classification Summer cooler

Planter's Punch

This is equally good as an aperitif before dinner or as a long drink, in summer or winter.

2 apples
2 pears
½ lemon
½ orange
2 peaches
2 bottles red wine
2 sherry glasses of port or other heavy red wine
½ pint (1¼ cups) diluted lime juice
crushed ice

Peel and cut up the fruit, discarding all the damaged areas, cores, pips and pith. Skin and slice the peaches. Put all the fruit into a bowl and add half the red wine. Cover the bowl with a tea towel and leave for six hours in a cool place (not a refrigerator). Just before serving add the remainder of the red wine, the port and the lime juice. Stir gently. Serve the ice separately.

Classification Summer cooler

Sangria

A common drink in Spain and Portugal with meals. Looks very attractive on the table. Keep a spare jug full in reserve!

---

1 bottle red wine
½ lemon sliced, with peel
½ orange sliced, with peel
1 tablespoon white sugar

Put all the ingredients together in a glass jug 2 or 3 hours before it will be used. Stir to dissolve the sugar and put in the refrigerator. Add ice lumps before serving.

Classification Summer cooler

Fruit Wine Cup

1 bottle orange wine
2 small measures brandy or whisky
1 small can mandarin oranges
1 small bottle dry cider
sugar
strawberries, raspberries or blackcurrants

Mix the orange wine and spirits, add the strained juice from the mandarin oranges. Leave to chill in the refrigerator. Just before serving, stir in the cider and add sugar to taste. Add ice, mandarin oranges and soft fruit and mix gently, then serve.

Classification Summer cooler

Summer Cup

¼ pint (⅝ cup) lemon squash
¼ pint (⅝ cup) orange squash
1 bottle damson or elderberry wine
4 tablespoons (5 T) sugar
cracked ice
2 peaches, sliced
1 orange, sliced
½ lb. (1⅓ cups) strawberries, halved
4 oz. (⅔ cup) raspberries
1 pint (2½ cups) soda water
slices of cucumber to decorate

Add the fruit squashes to the wine in a bowl. Stir in the sugar until it has dissolved and pour this mixture over lumps of cracked ice in a punch-bowl. Add the fruits. Just before serving, add the soda water. Serve in tall glasses with a thin slice of cucumber fixed to the rim of the glass.

Classification Summer cooler

Spiced Cider

1 bottle cider
3 tablespoons (3¾ T) honey
1 lemon
1 teaspoon cinnamon

Dissolve the honey in the cider, then add the other ingredients while warming up.

Classification Winter warmer

Gluwein

This is a delicious heart-warming apres-ski drink from Austria.

1 bottle red wine
½ tablespoon sugar
1 packet (or as directed) of mulled spices

Coffee rum punch (left)

Warm all the ingredients together in a saucepan, with the spices in a muslin bag. Do not overheat. Serve immediately.

Classification Winter warmer

Rum Punch

Rum punches can be made using a dry Hock type of white wine instead of red wine. Another variation is Tea Punch. Freshly made hot tea is added to the mixture instead of water; or you can use half tea and half boiling water.

2 lemons
½ lb. (1 cup) lump sugar
1 pint (2½ cups) red wine (claret type is best)
¾ pint (1⅞ cups) rum
1 pint (2½ cups) boiling water

Rub the zest from the lemon rind with a few lumps of sugar, then put all the sugar in a pan with the red wine and rum and bring to the boil. Extract the juice from the lemons and strain it. When the sugar has melted and the mixture has boiled, add the boiling water and the lemon juice. Mix well and serve hot. You can serve this punch cold if preferred—cool in the saucepan with the lid on.

Classification Winter warmer

Summer punch

Elderberry Punch

juice and thinly peeled rind of 1 lemon
1 pint (2½ cups) elderberry wine
2 oz. (¼ cup) demerara sugar
½ pint (1¼ cups) cold water
4 cloves
3-inch stick cinnamon
root ginger (about 1-inch square)

Put all the ingredients in a saucepan and bring slowly to boiling point. Hold at this temperature for five minutes, then pour into a punch bowl. Serve hot.

Classification Winter warmer

Elderberry Wine Cup

juice and rind of 4 oranges
juice and rind of 2 lemons
1 teaspoon cloves
3-inch stick cinnamon
2 bottles elderberry wine

Use only the yellow parts of the orange and lemon rinds. Place these, the juices, cloves, cinnamon and wine in a tall jug. Leave to stand for two hours in a warm place. Strain through a nylon sieve into a saucepan. Heat to boiling point, but do not boil. Serve hot.

Classification Winter warmer

Coffee Rum Punch

8 lumps sugar
grated rind of 2 oranges
½ pint (1¼ cups) red wine
1 liqueur glass or miniature bottle rum
4-inch stick cinnamon
6–8 cups hot, strong black coffee

Put the sugar in a saucepan. Add the grated rind of the oranges, cover with the red wine and leave until the sugar has absorbed the wine. Then add the rum and cinnamon. Stir gently over a low heat. Add the hot strong coffee and serve at once.

Classification Winter warmer

Christmas Punch

1 bottle home-made red wine
1 glass cherry brandy (miniature bottle)
1 lemon, sliced
¼ teaspoon grated nutmeg
4 tablespoons (5 T) granulated sugar
2 oz. clear honey
½ pint (1¼ cups) boiling water
2 oz. (¼ cup) glacé cherries, halved

Heat the wine but do not boil it; add the cherry brandy, sliced lemon and nutmeg, stir in the sugar and honey until sugar dissolves. Add the boiling water and glacé cherries to the punch. Serve hot, at once, in tall glasses, making sure that there are a few cherry halves in each glass.

Classification Winter warmer
130

Party Mull

This is an inexpensive punch, ideal for sipping at a lively party at home. The quantities of wine and water can be adjusted as preferred.

1 bottle red wine
2 tablespoons (2½ T) clear honey
2 tablespoons (2½ T) sugar, brown or white
¾ teaspoon grated nutmeg
¾ teaspoon powdered cinnamon
1 pint (2½ cups) hot water
small can mixed fruit salad

Heat the wine and honey, add the sugar and stir until the sugar is dissolved. Add the spices, hot water and then the fruit salad. Serve very hot.

Classification Winter warmer

Mulled Cider

⅓ pint (⅜ cup) lemon squash
⅓ pint (⅜ cup) water
4 cloves
⅓ pint (⅜ cup) orange squash
2 tablespoons (2½ T) sugar
1 lemon, sliced
½ teaspoon powdered cinnamon
1 pint (2½ cups) cider
½ teaspoon grated nutmeg

Put all the ingredients except the cider and nutmeg into a saucepan and bring slowly to the boil. Add the cider and re-heat but do not boil. Strain into a warmed bowl and top with grated nutmeg.

Classification Winter warmer

Dr. Johnson's Choice

This mulled wine dates from 18th century England and was said to be the favourite of Dr. Samuel Johnson, the writer and lexicographer.

1 bottle red wine
12 lumps sugar
¼ teaspoon grated nutmeg
¼ teaspoon ground cinnamon
½ pint (1¼ cups) boiling water
1 tablespoon (1¼ T) brandy

Pour the wine into a punch bowl, add the sugar and spices and heat, but do not boil. Then add the boiling water and mix well. Lastly add the brandy. You may vary the amount of brandy according to taste or pocket!

Classification Winter warmer

Making elderberry wine cup

Apricot Mull

Ordinary brandy (cognac) can be used instead of apricot brandy if you wish, aad more spice and fruit can be added according to taste.

1 bottle red wine (burgundy type)
2 glasses apricot brandy
3 cloves
¼ teaspoon grated nutmeg
squeeze of lemon juice
1 tablespoon (1¼ T) brown sugar
slice of lemon

Put all the ingredients in a saucepan, heat to boiling point but do not boil. Pour into a glass jug and float a slice of lemon on top.

Classification Winter warmer

Bishop's Nightcap

3 or 4 cloves
1 sweet orange
spices—cinnamon, nutmeg, mace, root ginger
¼ pint (⅝ cup) water
½ bottle red wine
2 oz. (¼ cup) loaf sugar
1 lemon

Stick the cloves in the orange and roast it in front of the fire, or bake in the oven. Put small quantities of the spices (according to taste) in a pan with the water and boil for five minutes. Heat the wine but do not boil it, then add the roasted orange, the sugar that has been rubbed on the lemon rind, and the juice of the lemon. Leave by the fire or on a stove over a low heat for 10 minutes. Strain, add a grating of nutmeg and serve piping hot.

Classification Winter warmer

White Wine Rum Punch

2 lemons
½ lb. (1 cup) lump sugar
1 pint (2½ cups) dry white wine (a hock type)
¾ pint (1⅞ cups) rum
1 pint (2½ cups) boiling water

Rub the zest from the lemon peel with a few lumps of sugar, then put all the sugar in a pan with the white wine and rum and bring to the boil. Extract the juice from the lemons and strain it. When the sugar has melted and the mixture comes to the boil, add the boiling water and lemon juice.

Mix well and serve hot. If preferred, you can leave this punch to stand in the saucepan, with the lid on, and serve cold.

Classification Winter warmer

Mulled Ale (1)

Brandy may be substituted for the rum.

1 quart (1⅕ quarts) ale or light beer
6 cloves
a piece of root ginger
¼ nutmeg
1 dessertspoon (1 T) honey or brown sugar
1 glass rum

Put the ale, spices and honey or sugar in a saucepan, bring to boiling point and simmer (do not boil) for a few minutes. Strain, add the rum and serve at once.

Classification Winter warmer

Mulled Ale (2)

Again, brandy may be substituted for the rum, if preferred.

1 quart (1⅕ quarts) ale or light beer
1 dessertspoon (1 T) clear honey
6 cloves
piece of root ginger
¼ nutmeg, grated
1 glass rum

Put the ale, honey and spices in a pan, bring to boiling point and simmer for two to three minutes. Strain, add the rum and serve at once.

Classification Winter warmer

A mulled wine looks and tastes good

Cooking with Wine and Beer

Most wines can be successfully added to both cooked and uncooked foods, resulting in improved flavour and, sometimes, appearance. As examples of what can be done, there are a number of recipes in this chapter, showing the use of differing wines in the preparation of appropriate dishes.

Or you may wish to try a favourite recipe that calls for an imported, commercial wine, substituting a home-made wine of comparable character. However, you should bear in mind, as with most aspects of wine making and consumption, that individual taste is the deciding factor.

Indeed, if you are feeling adventurous, instead of modifying an established recipe by degrees and in the light of experience, you may wish to follow the general-ised notes below.

Soup Red wine in darker soups and white wine in cream soups or consommés makes a delicious addition; it really lifts them out of the ordinary and makes, often, a good conversational start to the meal. The quantity used should be about a cupful of wine per pint. Alternatively, about half this quantity of dry sherry can be added to almost any soup, with advantage. Add the wine or sherry after boiling up, or else the alcohol will be lost, but continue heating for a little while otherwise the soup may be overcooled.

Gravies The same remarks apply as for soups.

Roasts Many cooks pour a glass or two of red wine over beef or lamb, or white wine over chicken or veal, while roasting. The high temperature will evaporate the alcohol, but the flavour of the wine will remain.

Casseroles The addition of red wine to beef, and white to veal, lamb or chicken casseroles will really transform their taste. The aroma of the wine pervades right through the dish. About a cupful per pint will do, but this quantity can always be adjusted to taste. A bottle of light ale to a casserole is an unusual, but very pleasant, addition to a beef dish. Add the wine or beer before cooking commences.

Baked Fish If you like fish baked in milk, try adding half a glass of white wine, during cooking.

Marinades Beef and some fish can be marinated in wine, and spices if liked, for several hours before cooking.

Cakes Brown ale, or stout is, of course, a common ingredient to the heavier, fruity cakes, especially Christmas cakes. Ensure that you follow the cake recipe, which will have been carefully balanced to achieve the correct amount of moisture.

Fruit Salads Try a glass of raisin wine poured over a mixed fruit salad, or a sweetish red wine over a bowl of strawberries or raspberries. Alternatively, soak the strawberries in the wine for an hour or two before serving, and sprinkle the berries with a small quantity of castor sugar.

Trifles Soak the sponge cakes in a strong, raisin flavoured wine, or sherry, before adding the other ingredients. Wine gives a delicious tang to any trifle.

Add some home-made white wine when cooking fish

Mussels in White Wine

1 quart mussels
chopped parsley
1 small onion, chopped
chopped clove garlic (if liked)
1 teaspoon softened butter
salt and pepper
1 bottle white wine

Wash the mussels thoroughly, in several waters, rejecting any that are open. (Open-shelled mussels are not fresh and therefore dangerous.)

Put the cleaned mussels in a deep saucepan and sprinkle with parsley, onion and garlic. Add butter, salt, pepper and wine to cover and boil for 15 minutes with the lid firmly closed. When all the mussels are open, they are cooked; any that remain closed after this time should not be eaten.

Serve the mussels in their shells in soup plates; place the liquor—into which they should be dipped—in separate small dishes or cups.

Duck with Orange

sage and onion stuffing
1 × 3 lb. duckling
$\frac{1}{2}$ pint ($1\frac{1}{4}$ cups) orange wine
2 medium-sized oranges
1 teaspoon cornflour

Put the stuffing in the body of the bird. Place the duckling in an enamel or stoneware (*not* metal) baking dish. Pour the wine over the bird.

Slice one orange into sections, leaving the skin on. Lay the slices along the top of the bird, allowing them to overlap a little. Cover with foil and roast in a fairly hot oven (375°F, 195°C, Gas Mark 5) for one and a half hours, basting with the wine in the dish every 20 minutes. For the last 15 minutes, remove the foil and the orange slices, to allow the bird to brown. Slice the remaining orange and poach the slices in the liquor in the baking tin.

When cooked, take out the duck and place it on a serving dish. Arrange the orange slices around the edge of the dish. (The slices that have been cooked with the duck can also be used if they are not too broken.)

Pour off the liquor in the baking tin into a small saucepan, making it up to half a pint ($1\frac{1}{4}$ cups) if necessary with more wine. Put on to boil. Mix the cornflour to a smooth paste with a little wine; when the wine in pan is boiling, pour it over the blended cornflour, stirring well. Return all to the pan and bring to the boil over a low heat, stirring all the time. Pour into a sauce or gravy boat. Serve slices of orange with each portion and the orange sauce separately.

As duck is naturally a fat bird, it is not necessary to add extra fat in roasting. If necessary, add more orange wine during cooking.

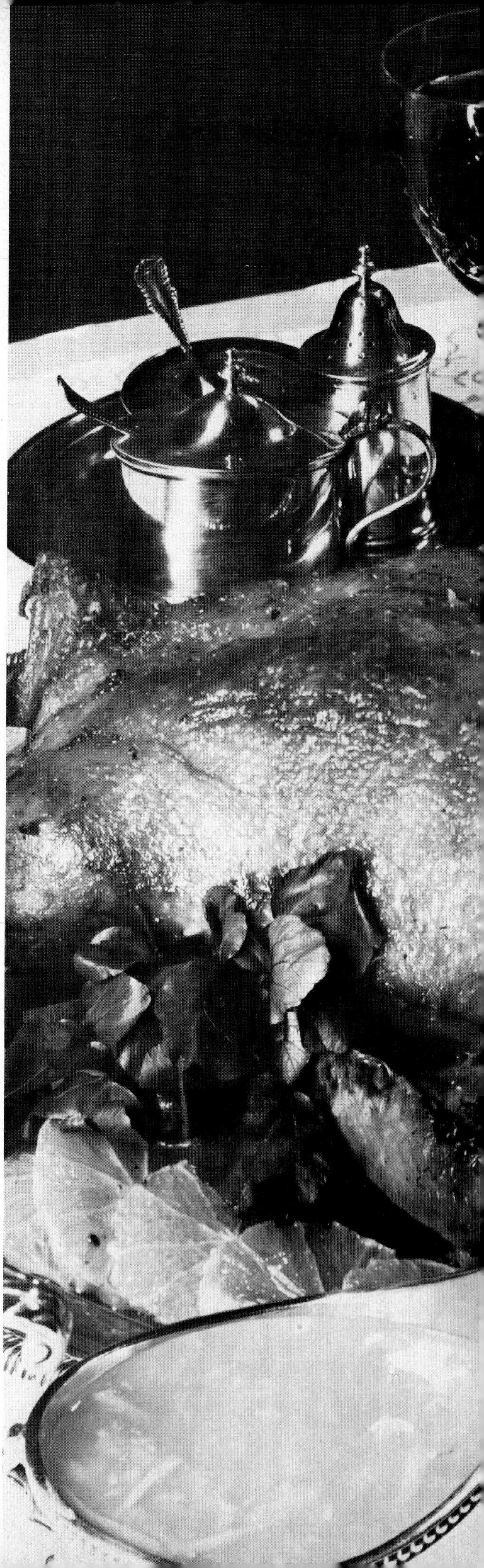

Duck with orange

Braised Beef

2 lb. topside or top rump of beef
salt and pepper
1 dessertspoon (1 T) flour
1 teaspoon dry mustard
2 oz. (¼ cup) dripping or lard (fat)
⅓ pint (⅞ cup) parsnip wine

Wipe the meat dry with a towel. Mix ½ teaspoon salt and a good sprinkling of pepper with the flour and the dry mustard. Cover the lean sides of the beef with this, let it stand for 15 minutes or so, then shake to remove surplus flour.

Heat the dripping or lard (fat) in a thick pan and fry the beef until lightly browned on both lean sides. Place in an ovenware dish with a lid, or in a casserole. Pour in the wine, cover closely and braise in a slow oven (300°F, 149°C, Gas Mark 2) for three and a half to four hours. Set the meat, with juices, on a serving dish.

Sautéed Lambs' Kidneys

6 lambs' or sheeps' kidneys
1 oz. (2 T) butter
1 tablespoon (1¼ T) flour
1 tablespoon (1¼ T) stock or gravy
salt and pepper
⅓ pint (⅞ cup) parsnip wine

Skin the kidneys and cut them in thin slices lengthways, removing the cores.

Melt the butter in a thick pan, and brown the kidneys lightly on both sides (two to three minutes each side). Set them on a hot serving dish. Stir the flour, stock and salt and pepper to taste into the butter and juices remaining in the frying pan. When smooth, cook, stirring all the time, for two to three minutes. Then pour in the wine, stir until boiling again and simmer for three minutes, stirring all the time. Pour this sauce over the kidneys and serve.

Veal in Red Wine

1 lb. breast of veal
4 oz. chopped fat bacon
1 small onion, chopped
1 dessertspoon (1 T) chopped celery
1 green pepper, chopped
⅓ pint (⅞ cup) beetroot wine
2 tablespoons (2½ T) tomato sauce
¼ pint (⅝ cup) veal stock (a meat cube can be used)

Cut the veal into pieces, removing any skin or gristle. Lightly fry the chopped bacon, onion, celery and green pepper. When all are lightly browned, add the veal and

Sautéed lambs' kidneys

cook, stirring to prevent sticking, until the veal is browned. Then add the wine, cover the pan and simmer for 30 minutes, stirring two or three times. When the liquid is very much reduced, add the tomato sauce and stock and stir until boiling again. Reduce heat and stir until sauce thickens.

Fondue

1 clove garlic
4 wine glasses light white wine
¾ lb. Emmenthal cheese
¾ lb. Gruyere cheese
1 heaped teaspoon cornflour
1 liqueur glass Kirsch
little grated nutmeg
little cayenne pepper
crusty French loaf

Rub the inside of an earthenware casserole with a cut clove of garlic and leave the garlic pieces in it. Pour in the wine and heat it over a low flame. Add the thinly sliced cheese, a slice at a time, stirring all the time until it has melted. When the cheese begins to bubble, add the cornflour and Kirsch and mix to a smooth paste. Season with a pinch of grated nutmeg and a dash of cayenne pepper.

Stand the fondue on a spirit stove or chafing dish over a very low heat so that it keeps hot without actually boiling. Then put the fondue on the table and cut the French bread into small squares. Each diner is now supplied with a very long fork so that he can spear the pieces of French bread and dip them into the fondue, taking up the tasty cheese mixture.

If Kirsch is not obtainable, gin or brandy may be used. In Switzerland, where eating fondue and drinking wine mark great social occasions, the correct wine in fondues is Neuchatel, but for home wine-makers, your own dry white wine may be used both in the cooking and for drinking. As an accompaniment to fondue, dry white wine or milkless tea is considered correct by the Swiss and a small glass of Kirsch is usually served halfway through the meal.

Compote of Rhubarb

1 lb. young rhubarb
3 tablespoons (3¾ T) water
2 tablespoons (2½ T) sugar
3 tablespoons (3¾ T) elderberry wine

Use only the red parts of the rhubarb. Wipe with a towel and cut it into 1-inch pieces. Make a syrup, in a saucepan, with the water and sugar, add the rhubarb and simmer until tender but unbroken. (You can cook this in the oven, in a covered casserole, if preferred.) By making a syrup of the sugar and water, there is less risk of the rhubarb breaking during cooking.

Add the wine and bring to boiling point again. Serve hot or cold.

Weights and Measurements

All measurements in this book are based on Imperial weights and measures. American equivalents, where different, are given in parenthesis.

Where a cup measurement is given, this refers to the American cup of 8 fluid ounce capacity.

Measurements in *weight* in the Imperial and American system are the same. Measurements in *volume* are different and the following table shows the equivalents:

Spoon measurements

Imperial	U.S.
1 teaspoon (5 ml)	$1\frac{1}{4}$ teaspoons
1 tablespoon (20 ml)	$1\frac{1}{4}$ tablespoons (abbrev.: T)

Liquid measurements

1 Imperial pint = 20 fluid ounces
1 American pint = 16 fluid ounces
1 American cup = 8 fluid ounces
1 Imperial gallon = 160 fluid ounces = 8 Imperial pints
1 American gallon = 133 fluid ounces
1 Imperial gallon = $1\frac{1}{5}$ American gallons

Metric measurements

The following are approximate metric equivalents:
45 grams = $1\frac{1}{2}$ oz.
500 grams = 1 lb. $1\frac{1}{2}$ oz.
1 kilogram = 2 lb. 3 oz.
10 fluid oz. = 285 ml.

To convert	into	multiply by
pounds	kilograms	0·45
ounces	grams	28·3
fluid ounces	millilitres	23
kilograms	pounds	2·2
grams	ounces	0·035
litres	pints	1·76

Glossary of terms

Aerobic fermentation
Fermentation in the atmosphere, i.e. the vessel is not fully sealed.

Alcohol
Obtained by the fermentation of sugar by the enzymes in yeast.

Anaerobic fermentation
Fermentation within a vessel sealed with a trap or air lock.

Attenuation
The lowering of the specific gravity of the wort by fermentation.

Balance
The correct proportions of sweetness, flavour, acidity and alcohol in a wine.

Blending
Mixing wines of differing qualities, e.g. an over-acid wine with an insipid one to a palatable result.

Body
A cowslip wine may have no body to speak of; an elderberry or blackcurrant will have plenty.

Calcium sulphate
A useful additive to harden water.

Campden tablets
A convenient form of sodium metabisulphite – see **Sulphur dioxide**.

Caramel
Colouring agent for beers and stouts. Obtained by heating sugar until it darkens.

Carbon dioxide
The gas (harmless) given off by fermenting wine.

Condition
Assessment of a beer by the amount of carbon dioxide gas present.

Dextrin
A starch gum used to give body and persistent 'head' to beer.

Dry
A wine in which all the sugar has been converted into alcohol or 'fermented right out'.

Fermentation
The conversion of sugar into alcohol, brought about by yeast enzymes.

Fermentation trap
A water-sealed airlock or 'bubbler' fitted to the fermentation vessel during anaerobic fermentation.

Fining
Clearing wine or beer of cloudiness.

Finings
Isinglass, beaten white of egg, Bentonite and many proprietary liquids or powders, used for clearing.

Flogger
A wooden corking tool.

Fortification
The addition of spirits to wine.

Glucose
A sweetening agent (dextrose) obtained from starch.

Grist
Generic name for grains used for beer mash.

Head
The foam on top of a glass of beer.

Hydrometer
A weighted, calibrated, glass float used to indicate the specific gravity of the wine or beer.

Invert Sugar
Treated sugar – gives a quicker fermentation than cane sugar.

Isinglass
Mainly gelatin, obtained from fish bladders. Used as finings.

Lactose
Milk sugar, less sweet than cane sugar. Unfermentable, so used to sweeten dark beers and stouts.

Lees (beer)
Dead yeast and vegetable debris that settles on the bottom of a fermentation vessel or floats to the top.

Lees (wine)
Dead yeast and vegetable sediment in bottom of fermenting or storage jar.

Liquor
Brewer's name for the water used in beer making.

Magnesium sulphate
A useful additive to soften water.

Malt
Barley after heating in moist atmosphere, just beginning to sprout. The starch in the barley is by now converted to maltose. Further growth is prevented by drying the grains.

Malt extract
Syrup obtained by evaporating the wort.

Mash
The boiled-up malted grains.

Must
The unfermented, pulped, ingredients of the wine: also the strained juice therefrom.

Pitching temperature
The wort temperature (60°F, 15·5°C) at which the yeast should be added.

Priming sugar
Sugar added just before bottling to induce a secondary fermentation so that the beer is gassy.

Racking
Siphoning off clear wine or beer into another vessel, leaving behind the lees.

Rousing
Vigorous stirring of the beer during fermentation.

Sulphur dioxide
Sterilizing and preserving gas given off by Campden tablets and sodium metabisulphite. Added to the must of wine, or put into empty vessels, it kills bacteria.

Vinometer
A glass gauge for measuring the alcoholic content of wine.

Wort
The liquor drained off the mash.

Index

Acknowledgments

The following black and white photographs by courtesy of:
Bernard Alfieri 22 above and below, 23, 24, 84 centre and
below Barnaby's Picture Library 38–39, 93 Boots and Co.
Ltd. 25 above right Bulmer's Cider Press 92 Good
Housekeeping 22 centre, 24–25, 26 above right and below
Melvin Grey 4–5 Heals Ltd 101 W. R. Loftus Ltd. 18, 19
above right and below Mansell Collection 56–57, 104–105,
115 Mary Evans Picture Library 35, 98 Dick Miller 8–9,
12–13, 21, 29, 30–31, 46–47, 51, 63, 71, 102–103, 110-111,
118, 126–127, 131 PAF International Ltd. 135 Popperfoto
6–7, 40 John C. Seed/British Oxygen Co. 107 all, 108 all, 109
all M. A. Snelgrove 10, 12 Syndication International 19 above
left, 25 top left, 26 top left, 52 all, 84 above, 132, 137, 138

The following colour transparencies by courtesy of:
Angel Studios 44, 129 Robert Estall 36 above John Gay 116
above Good Housekeeping 36 below, 80, 91 Melvin Grey 2–3
John Lee 15, 48, 65, 68, 69, 73, 82 top, 82–83, 87, 113, 116
below, 121, 124 below, 128 The Picture Library 125 John C.
Seed/British Oxygen Co. 116–117 Spectrum 11 Standbrook
Publications 124 above Syndication International 33, 37,
40–41, 45, 82 below, 120 Tom Caxton Beer Kits 94–95

Line Illustrations: by Barrington Barber (1, 42, 43, 54, 55, 58,
59, 60, 66, 67, 78, 79) by Mary Tomlin (14, 16–17, 20, 28, 90,
96, 100, 106, 112, 134)

Jacket illustrations: Syndication International
Endpapers and jacket flaps: Melvin Grey

The publishers would like to thank Loftus Ltd. for the wine
and beer making equipment which they kindly loaned for use
in photography.

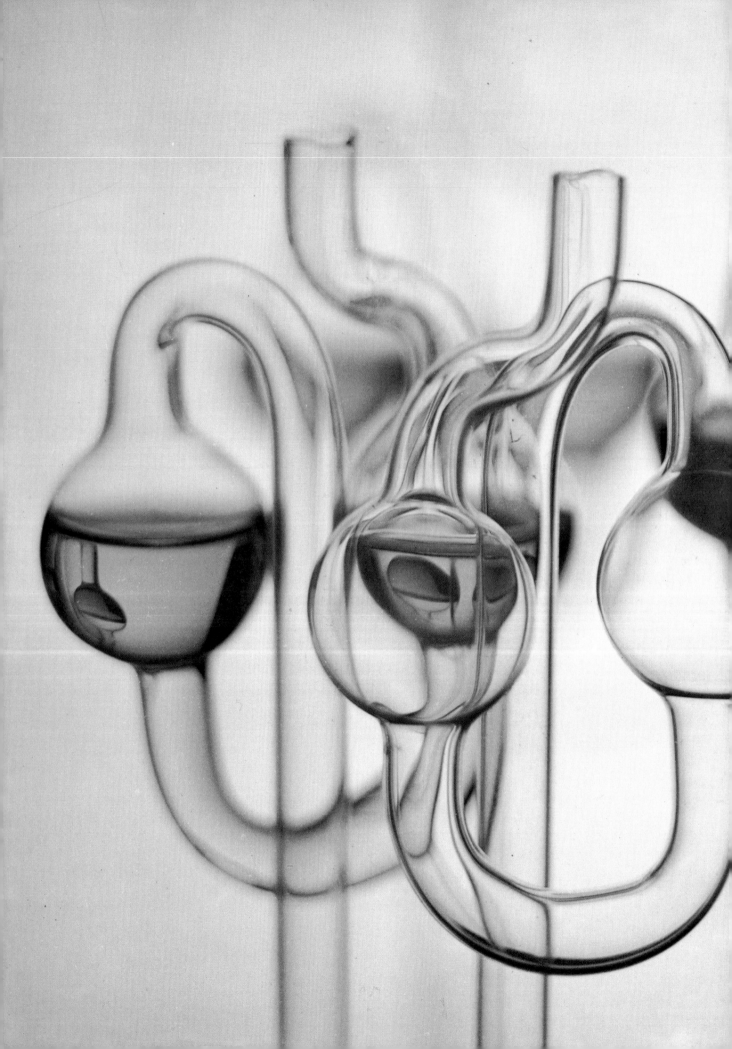